P9-ANZ-181

TRAINING DELIVERY SKILLS: II MAKING THE TRAINING DELIVERY

Robert R. Carkhuff and Richard M. Pierce

With

John R. Cannon

Sharon G. Fisher

Ted W. Friel

CARNEGIE LIBRARY
LIVINGSTONE COLLEGE
SALISBURY, N. C. 28144

Copyright © 1984 by
Human Resource Development Press, Inc.

22 Amherst Rd.
Amherst, Massachusetts 01002 (413) 253-3488

Bernice R. Carkhuff, Publisher

All rights reserved. Printed in the United States of America. No part of the material protected by this copyright notice may be reproduced or utilized in any form or by any means, electronic or mechanical, including photocopying, recording, or by information storage and retrieval system without written permission from the copyright owner.

First Edition, Second Printing, November, 1985

Library of Congress Cataloging in Publication Data
International Standard Book Number 0-914234-74-9

Cover Art by Krawczyk
Cover Design by Tom Bellucci
Composition by The Magazine Group
Printing and Binding by Bookcrafters

658.3124
C277

Table of Contents

118800

About the Authors

Robert R. Carkhuff, Ph.D., Chairman, Carkhuff Institute of Human Technology, Amherst, Massachusetts, is among the most-cited social scientists according to the Institute for Scientific Information. He is author of three of the most-referenced social science texts, including two volumes on *Helping and Human Relations.* His latest books are *Sources of Human Productivity* and *The Exemplary Performer in the Age of Productivity.*

Richard M. Pierce, Ph.D., Director, Human Resource Development, Human Technology, Inc., McLean, Virginia, has designed the implementation programs for more than 500 projects in the last 15 years. He is co-author of a forthcoming book on *Performance Management Systems.*

John R. Cannon, Ph.D., Director, Management Systems, Human Technology, Inc., McLean, Virginia, has directed more than 600 projects in the last 12 years. He is co-author of a forthcoming book on *The Art and Science of Consulting.*

Sharon G. Fisher, M.Ed., Director, Instructional Systems Design, Human Technology, Inc., McLean, Virginia, has designed hundreds of public and private sector instructional projects and products. She is recipient of the first "Exemplar Award" for her exemplary products in C.A.I. as well as print material.

Ted W. Friel, Ph.D., Director, Advanced Systems Design, Human Technology, Inc., McLean, Virginia, has done operations planning for more than 400 projects in the last 14 years. He is author of *The Art of Developing a Career* and co-author of a forthcoming book on *Human Resource Planning.*

Foreword

In 1969, Carkhuff wrote the now landmark, *Helping and Human Relations*. Hailed as a classic in its time, it defined the operations of both counseling and training for the first time in human history.

In 1971, Carkhuff followed with the monumental *The Development of Human Resources*. Focusing upon education and training as the vehicles to human resource development, it operationalized the "human" goal in human resource development.

During the ensuing decade, Carkhuff and his associates developed the blueprint for education and the technologies for its teaching and learning skills. Written for teachers in 1981, *The Skilled Teacher* became a standard for trainers and developers in both the private and public sectors.

Now, based upon the extensive empirical evidence of hundreds of instructional design and productivity improvement efforts in business and government, Carkhuff and his associates bring us a package of volumes on *Instructional Systems Design* and *Training Delivery Skills*. I will focus upon the latter in my review.

I myself have been trained in the systems and skills of Carkhuff's "human technology." I have successfully utilized the models and technologies in my daily work efforts as a trainer, developer and manager of trainers and developers. These programs have produced dramatically positive results in terms of the performance of trainers, the productivity of training units and, above all, the productivity of the final recipients of these programs.

In considering training delivery skills, it is important to emphasize that our instructional design efforts are necessary but not sufficient conditions of our training deliveries. Our design efforts occur prior to contact with the trainees. How we implement the designs in interaction with the trainees dictates the effectiveness of our training efforts.

In this context, *Training Delivery Skills* teaches us the training delivery skills we need to make a successful training delivery. Volume I emphasizes the skills we need to prepare the training delivery. These preparation skills emphasize developing and organizing the training content, taking the trainees into consideration. They culminate in a training plan for managing the learning of the trainees.

Volume II teaches the critical skills for making a training delivery. These training delivery skills emphasize two sets of skills: 1) those involved in processing the trainees in terms of the requirements of the content; and 2) those involved in processing the content in terms of the trainees' experiences. That is, the trainers teach content! And they also teach trainees!

These critical training delivery skills are complemented by the training transfer skills necessary to insure transfer to the world of work. They are also supplemented by the training evaluation skills necessary to make assessments of our training efforts.

Training Delivery Skills is most valuable in a pre-service context where prospective trainers are being trained. It incorporates the very training skills in which the candidates are being trained: defining the training skill objectives; developing the skill content; developing the training delivery plan; and making the training delivery. It is also valuable for experienced trainers and instructional designers for purposes of programmatically reviewing or learning the training skills they were never taught. In this context, it may be fruitfully used in conjunction with the series on *Instructional Systems Design.*

To sum, *Training Delivery Skills* is a valuable text for all instructional personnel. It teaches training skills by a simple, step-by-step method. It emphasizes the all-too-often neglected training process between trainer and trainees. Our training effectiveness begins with our content and interpersonal processing skills. In the end, we are as effective as we are knowledgeable in our training content and skilled in our training delivery.

For delivering to us these training preparation and delivery skills, we owe Carkhuff and his associates a great debt of gratitude. For delivering to our clients our specialty contents, we owe our clients our best productivity efforts based upon those training delivery skills made available to us by Carkhuff and his associates.

Ed Feder, Manager
Training and Organizational Development
AMOCO Production Company
Standard Oil of Indiana

Preface

The aftermath of an exhaustive study of performance-based supervision is relevant. Conducted by a Fortune 100 corporation, the study was three years in the making and cost millions of dollars—much greater resource expenditures than most organizations can make. Yet within weeks, we incorporated hypotheses generated by this study into our own supervisory training design. In other words, we tested its hypotheses "on a shoe string." We found very different results: interpersonal processing or facilitation skills rather than supervisory "survival" skills such as planning and controlling were prepotent.

The point is that by the time the initial study was in print, its results were already modified. This finding is an analogue of the Information Age: because of the changing data, everything is changing quickly. Instructional design and training delivery programs must become flexible and quickly responsive striking forces. We simply can no longer afford to design training programs that are obsolete by the time we deliver them. Succinctly, trainers and developers need "hip pocket" skills that enable them to design and implement instructional systems "on their feet," fluidly and potently in the moment of need for these systems. The volumes on *Training Delivery Skills* are dedicated to meet this need.

January 1984
Washington, D.C.

R.R.C. and R.M.P.

I

INTRODUCTION AND OVERVIEW

Human learning or processing is the basis for all training and development. The training content must be developed to facilitate the trainees' naturalistic learning styles. The training delivery must facilitate the trainees' movement through the learning or training process: exploring where they are in relation to the training experience; understanding their training goals for where they want or need to be; acting upon training programs to achieve their training goals.

PHASES OF TRAINING

▶EXPLORING ───▶ UNDERSTANDING ───▶ ACTING

| Trainees' experiences | Trainees' goals | Upon training programs |

I

Learning and Development in the Age of Information

The most profound changes to take place in the Age of Information are those in human processing. Dominated as they were by the conditioning programs of the Industrial Age, people are not accustomed to processing the expanding information that now presses them so fully. People need to acquire generic processing skills. They need to know how to process personally: to explore, understand, and act upon the information they have received. They need to know how to process interpersonally: to facilitate the exploring, understanding, and acting of others.

In the Industrial Age, personnel were valued for their conditioned response "grooves," i.e., the specific responses which they acquired to specific stimuli over a period of time. The process of conditioning, while often taking many years, was not totally uneconomical because the personnel could utilize the responses for many more years. Since the information input was relatively constant and often isolated, the few responses which personnel acquired over their lifetimes would suffice to serve them and their organizations. Indeed, "the man" controlled the organizational hierarchy by controlling the information flow, disseminating only that knowledge essential for his organizational purposes.

While there is a place for this conditioned responding in the Age of Information, it is limited by the few mechanical tasks performed by humans that await their replacement by machines. The information input is no longer stable and isolated. It is instead constantly changing and universal. This change is the great difference between the two ages. Digital and communication techniques have converged upon one common mission: the unimpeded flow of global information. "The man" can control neither the information nor the organization in the same conditioned manner. More information flows across the average manager's desk in a week than was made available to a Carnegie or a Rockefeller in a lifetime. Accordingly, the nature of the relationships has changed dramatically. Each individual in an organization is interdependent with every other individual. Each must process the assigned mission in conjunction with the daily developing data and produce the most productive response, i.e., the response that generates the greatest results outputs while investing minimal resource inputs. The essential mission of the Age of Information is *interdependent processing for increasingly productive purposes* (Carkhuff, 1983a, 1983b).

The role of training and development in actualizing this mission is clear. Education and training are the sources of more than eighty percent of projected human and information resource development. In turn, human and information resource development are the sources of nearly one hundred percent of the productivity growth that comes increasingly to dominate economic growth (Carkhuff and

Pierce, 1984). Accordingly, the essential mission of training and development is to *facilitate the human and computer processing that develops human and information resources.*

To accomplish their human and information resource development mission, productive training and development personnel must now be skilled in two critical areas of expertise:

- TECHNICAL PROCESSING SKILLS: Human and mechanical processing in relation to their technical specialties.
- TRAINING DELIVERY SKILLS: Training delivery preparation and implementation skills.

Before developing the training and delivery skills, we must learn about human processing or learning. Before learning about learning, we must understand the organizational and individual requirements that are being imposed upon personnel by the press of information.

Organizational Productivity

We have had very recent occasion to work with management of two of the world's largest corporations. Each is recognized universally as a prototype of the Industrial and Information Eras. One firm is recognized as a leader among the now-disappearing smokestack industries. The other is universally acclaimed as the leader of the information industry.

The "smokestack" industry management personnel are in fragmentation rather than transition to the requirements of the Information Age. Twenty years ago they were smug in their management philosophy and doctrinaire in their educational and training approaches. Indeed, it was precisely this attitude of smugness that led to their current problems. Now in the middle of a huge trough, and finding no easy way out, the personnel are honestly searching in an open-ended manner for a vision of new organizational productivity.

In turn, the information industry personnel are satisfied with their productivity and, to be sure, their share of the market. They have their own unique way of doing things and, based upon their past successes, they are doctrinaire in their education and training programs. Quite naturally, the troubled "smokestack" industry seeks to emulate the performance of the successful "information" industry. Indeed, the "information" agency is now duplicating the earlier management philosophy of the "smokestack" industry: one clear, monolithic thrust to the goal line with all personnel conditioned to that end.

The great paradox is that the "information" organization is itself in a pre-crisis stage, not unlike the "smokestack" organization was 20 years ago. The "smokestack" organization is merely among the earliest to be dashed upon the rocks of productivity. All organizations will face these problems within the next six months to a year and, then, in increasingly telescoped cycles thereafter. The increasingly doctrinaire approaches of the "information" organization, however historically data-based, sentence that organization to even greater productivity problems in the future.

A still greater paradox comes with the insight that the "information" industry has accommodated and met the requirements of the Electronics or Hardware Era through which we have just passed in the last 20 years. Indeed, it helped to set the standards. The problem is that its personnel are not disposed to preparing to enter the Information Age. In turn, the personnel of the "smokestack" industry are considering meeting the requirements of the Electronics Age through which we have already passed. Let us look at the differentiated requirements of the Industrial, Electronics, and Information Eras for both organizational

productivity and individual performance. Again, it is important to emphasize that the ingredients are developmental
and cumulative: the ingredients of an earlier era are incorporated in an increasingly diminished form in a later era.

Organizational productivity is defined by the components, functions, and processes that contribute to an organization's productivity, i.e., increasing its results outputs
while reducing its resource inputs. The components
emphasize the basic ingredients or building blocks of the
organization. The functions emphasize the basic functions
or purposes of the organization. The processes emphasize
the methods and procedures by which the organization
discharges the functions of its components (Carkhuff,
1983a) (see Table 1-1).

In terms of its components, we can see how the
resource components have shifted in emphasis from
capital- to systems- to people-based resources. In turn, production emphasis moves from machinery to computer
hardware to computer software. Perhaps one of the most
important changes is in the marketing component where
the movement is from manipulative "selling" through reac-
tive customer servicing to proactive efforts dedicated to
customer satisfaction, i.e., preventing the problems from
occurring and maximizing customer benefits. In turn, the
distribution shifts from ready-made commercial markets
through targeted multinational markets to universal markets. In short, the Information Age components shift to an
emphasis upon *human and information resource development dedicated to universal human satisfaction.*

The organizational functions are discharged by
dramatically different entities. In the Industrial Age, author-
itarian policy makers imposed narrow missions upon reac-
tive management planners, the plans to be enforced by rigid
supervisors and to be implemented by conditioned delivery
personnel. In the transitional Electronics Era, systems

Table 1-1
The Dimensions of Old, Transitional, and New Organizational Productivity

DIMENSIONS	ORGANIZATIONS		
	OLD (Industrial Era)	TRANSITION (Electronics Era)	NEW (Information Age)
COMPONENTS			
Resource	Capital	Systems	People
Production	Machinery	Computer Hardware	Computer Software
Marketing	Customer Sales	Customer Service	Customer Satisfaction
Distribution	Commercial Markets	Multinational Networks	Universal Markets
FUNCTIONS			
Policy	Authoritarian	Procedural	Data Based
Management	Reactive	Systematic	Interactive
Supervision	Enforcement	Monitored	Facilitative
Delivery	Conditioning	Mechanical Processing	Human Processing
PROCESSES			
Inputs	Raw Materials	Synthetics	Information
Outputs	Products	Services	Benefits
Processes	Machinery	Hardware	Software
Feedback	Random	Periodic	Constant

dominated as policy makers were procedural in defining their missions, managers were systematic in planning them, supervisors programmatic in monitoring the plans, and delivery personnel mechanical in the implementation of these plans.

Now, in the Information Age, the requirements are elevated geometrically. Policy and all other functions are data-based. Management is interactive in sharing its data bases—up, down, and sideways. Supervision is facilitative of delivery efforts which, themselves, increasingly emphasize human processing as the driver of the mechanical processing. In a very real sense, all personnel are in constant and productive revolution with the assigned missions: *based upon the data available to them, personnel are interactively designing and developing increasingly productive models to discharge their functions.*

The processes are a "quantum leap" different. During the Industrial Era, inputs emphasized seemingly infinite raw materials; outputs emphasized a seemingly endless array of survival, comfort, and luxury products; processes emphasized machinery-based processing that alleviated the burdens of physical drudgery; productivity feedback was, at best, random as we assumed the infinite nature of our resources.

The transitional Electronics Era marked changing emphases: to synthetic inputs and service outputs; to hardware processing and periodic samplings of productivity feedback. The transitional period was, nevertheless, preparatory for the requirements of the Information Age.

During the Information Age, information-based inputs are inversely related to all other resource inputs. In other words, the more information we have, the less resources we need. In turn, outputs are coming increasingly to emphasize not only customer but also human benefits, i.e., the positive outcomes of the services and products. The benefit ethic will drive the organizations independent of the original profit motive: those organizations that provide benefits survive and grow profitable. Clearly, an emphasis upon software-based processes increasingly escalates in a software "implosion" as software's productivity catches up with hardware's potential. Finally, the advances in hardware provide us the opportunity for constant productivity feedback. In short, *information-based inputs and processes are dedicated to humanly beneficial outputs.*

In summary, many Industrial Era businesses and industries are only now facing the requirements of the Age of Information. Unfortunately, many are viewing the systems requirements of the Electronics Era through which we have just passed rather than those that now confront us in sharp relief: *information-based components dedicated to processing-based functions implemented by people-based processes.*

Individual Performance

In working with the management personnel of two of the world's largest corporations, we came to several important conclusions. While less prepared, the personnel of the failing "smokestack" industry were open to meeting the requirements of the Information Age. In turn, while more prepared, the personnel of the successful "information" industry were closed to meeting the new requirements. Perhaps this is human nature: our successes and our failures, our strengths and our weaknesses are one and the same.

In any event, both sets of personnel require the energy, motivation, and intellect dedicated to meeting the challenges of the Information Age. Above all, they require the courage and integrity to commit the processing of their changing data inputs to improving their organization's productivity. Without constantly improving productivity, the organizations will go out of existence and the personnel will be useless: they will not know how to dedicate their individual performances to their organization's productivity.

We can see the great changes in individuals by analyzing their components, functions, and processes (see Table 1-2). The components emphasize the basic ingredients or composition of the individual. The functions emphasize the basic purposes or behaviors of the individual components. The processes emphasize the methods or enabling means to discharging the functions of the components.

We may view the changes in emphasis through three different periods: the old or Industrial Era; the transitional period or Electronics or Hardware Era; the new period or Information Age. Again, the emphasis upon the components, functions, and processes through the different eras is viewed as developmental and cumulative. Thus, for example, humans will continue to use conditioned habits for their economy of investment even while they are learning to think.

As can be seen, the components of an individual emphasize his or her physical, emotional, and intellectual makeup. During the Industrial Era, humans were seen physically as mechanical appendages to machinery. More recently, during the Hardware Age, humans have come to be seen as machines themselves. Now, during the Age of Information, we begin to view humans as humans, with the distinguishing human characteristic being the 100 billion neurons each of us possesses. Indeed, we view humans in terms of our latest, "state-of-the-art" machinery. We even describe our brain components in our latest scientific language: "Each neuron is programmed in chemical and electronic languages." To be sure, we now search to emulate the human condition by viewing machines as humans, i.e., having the potential to process in human-like ways.

Table 1-2
The Dimensions of Individual Performance in Different Eras

DIMENSIONS	OLD (Industrial Era)	INDIVIDUALS TRANSITION (Electronics Era)	NEW (Information Age)
COMPONENTS			
Physical	"Human as Mechanical Appendage"	"Human as Machine"	"Machine as Human Appendage"
Emotional	Dependent	Independent	Interdependent
Motivational	Incentives	Achievement	Actualization
Interpersonal	Top-Down	Lateral	Bottom-Up
Intellectual	Technologies	Systems	Models
FUNCTIONS			
Living	Orderly Living	Participative Living	Creative Living
Learning	Linear Thinking	Systems Thinking	Human Processing
Working	Corporate Obedience	Corporate Identification	Entrepreneurial Initiative
PROCESSES			
Exploring	Stimulus	Explore Experience	Analyze Dimensions
Understanding	No Understanding	Understand Goals	Operationalize Objectives
Acting	Response	Act Upon Programs	Technologize Programs

Emotionally, humans have moved in one human generation from emotional dependency (Industrial Era) through independency (Electronics Era) to a recognized need for interdependency in the Information Age. Interdependency emphasizes the systems dependency of each of us upon all of us. With a constantly changing data base, no one can control the information. Indeed, those closest to the phenomenon are most familiar with information relating to it. Thus, policy makers depend upon managers who depend upon supervisors who depend upon the delivery personnel. Interdependency is seen best in the teaching-learning process where each, in turn, is teacher of the other and learner from the other.

Motivationally, the changes in individual emphasis are similar. No longer do people work exclusively for external incentives as they did in the Industrial Age, nor do they work to satisfy their need to achieve or their pride in craftsmanship as in the transitional period. Now they work to actualize their resources in more and more productive efforts.

Interpersonally, people related historically in top-down relationships. The boss operated from a "give-and-go" basis: the supervisor gives the order and the subordinate goes out and performs the task. With transitional attention to lateral or peer relationships, people are now learning to operate from a bottom-up, "get, give, merge, and go" base: each *gets* and *gives* images, *merges* the images in the task to be performed, and *goes* out and does his or her part to complete the task. Thus, interpersonal relations in the Information Age define the interdependent relations of that age.

Intellectually, the individual's substance or specialty skills have changed in emphasis. During the Industrial Era, the individual developed simple, step-by-step linear technologies. During the Electronics Age, the individual realized the need for systems that integrate a number of variables at one time. Now in the Age of Information, the individual needs to be able to develop inclusive and operational models of substance in multidimensional space.

The individual functions may be summarized in living, learning, and working functioning. As can be seen, Industrial Era living functions emphasized orderly, top-down, "by-the-numbers" dependent relationships. In turn, Electronics Era living functions emphasized participative democracy in which children, students, and employees alike participated in designing goals for their own destinies. Now, the Information Age requires creative living: each individual is responsible for processing the entire data base and for making his or her own unique contributions to social good.

The learning functions emphasize the greatest differences between ages or eras. During the Industrial Age, the emphasis was upon linear thinking: making specific, step-by-step responses to specific, dimension-by-dimension stimuli. Indeed, schools were dominated by the memorization of linear responses and this memorization was conceived as the cornerstone of education. During the Electronics Era, individuals received training in systems thinking: the relating of variables and their interactions in time and space. To be sure, the great electronics breakthroughs like the microchip were products of the systems planning that coordinated these variables. The Age of Information requires human processing that produces multidimensional models that are quantitatively and qualitatively superior to the responses that stimulus materials were calculated to elicit, i.e., every response builds upon a creative integration of all previous responses.

The emphasis upon working functions shifts from corporate obedience in the Industrial Era through corporate identification in the Electronics Era to entrepreneurial initiative in the Information Age. Entrepreneurial initiative involves each individual at each performance station processing to improve his or her own individual performance as well as the unit's or organization's productivity.

The individual processes emphasize the exploring, understanding, and acting processes in which an individual engages. Exploring emphasizes the experiential relationship of individuals with stimulus experiences: *the individuals explore where they are in relation to the experience.* Understanding emphasizes the cognitive relationship of individuals with their response goals: *the individuals understand where they are in relation to where they want or need to be with their experience.* Acting emphasizes the behavioral relationship of individuals to their response programs: *the individuals act to get from where they are to where they want to be.*

During the Industrial Era, individuals were conditioned to make simple, straightforward responses to the stimuli. There was no need to understand their relationship with the goals for responding. They simply learned habitual, non-thinking responses.

During the Electronics Era, individuals participated in the processing of stimuli. They participated in exploring their experience in relation to the stimuli. They participated in understanding their relationship with their goals. They participated in acting upon their programs to achieve their goals.

Finally, during the Information Age, individuals are now required to engage in more productive cognitive processing: analyzing the dimensions of an experience or task; operationally defining the objectives for the experience or task; developing the technological programs to achieve the objectives. The demands are for increasingly sophisticated learning strategies and programs.

In summary, the changes in individual emphasis upon entry into the Age of Information are increasingly cognitive.

These changes call for us to learn the cognitive processing skills we require to process the daily changing data we receive. They require that we understand the learning processes that we seek to facilitate in order to become productive trainers and developers in the Age of Information.

Human Processing

Before we go on to learn about the training skills that facilitate learning, we should understand the learning process. Human growth and development involve some kind of a gain or change in human appearance or behavior. Human learning is the process by which this gain or change occurs (Ausebel, Novak and Havesian, 1978; Bloom, 1971; Dewey, 1910; Gagne, 1977; Guilford, 1967; Piaget, 1950, 1952; Piaget and Inhelder, 1969). In order for us to say that learning has occurred, then, there must be some kind of a demonstration of gain or change in behavior. The process out of which this learned behavior occurs can, but need not, be mediated by human intelligence. When it is not mediated by human intelligence, we say that the behavior was "conditioned." That is, the stimulus and response were associated and reinforced in such a way that either may evoke the other upon its appearance, without being processed by human intelligence.

When the behavior is mediated by human intelligence, we may say that true learning has occurred. That is, the learners were involved in a learning process that enabled them to use their intelligence in describing the causes, predicting the effects, and demonstrating the behavioral gain or change needed to achieve and use the effects. At the highest levels of intelligence, the learners are not only involved in such a learning process through the guidance of teachers; but they also become equipped with the learning-to-learn skills they need to involve themselves and move through the process.

Human processing depends upon how we develop our human resources. To this end, human processing depends upon how the environment—which is largely human—interacts with our biological selves. We can see this most clearly in the first year of a child's life. The newborn infant enters the world with little ability to relate to it other than through physiological reflex responses. For example, the child has the sucking reflex and the palmar or grasping reflex.

If the environment is responsive to the child, these reflexes will become instrumental to the child's survival. They constitute the child's initial movements toward the world which will lead, ultimately, to his or her growth and development. The child will be able to nurse with the sucking reflex. Later on, the child will be able to grasp things with the grasping reflex.

In the beginning, however, newborn infants bring little but their inherent resources to their worlds. In their utter dependency, they wait for us to insure their survival by responding to their needs, and by gradually guiding them to the things they need to have to maintain themselves.

One of the ways that we guide our children is by helping them to form habits. Basically, human habits are behaviors that are acquired without human intelligence. They can be acquired by associating or relating, in space and time, two or more sets of activities. At least one of these activities must satisfy some human need in order for the behavior to be repeated as a habit. For example, the child may develop the sucking habit when nourished by the mother's breast. The results may be said to be instrumental in satisfying the child's need for nourishment.

In the process, the child may develop a "conditioned" sucking response to the stimulus of the mother's nipple. In a similar manner, the child later on may develop a conditioned grasping response to the stimulus of food, which is instrumental in satisfying the child's need for nourishment. Many other kinds of life habits can be developed without human intelligence or intentionality.

The learning theorists write of these habits in terms of classical, instrumental, and other kinds of conditioning. The habits are "learned" only in the sense that they are repeated. They are not learned in the sense of being the product of human understanding. In fact, these habits are conditioned spinal responses, not learned responses. Indeed, most of what we teach about learning is based upon what we know about conditioning, which is precisely why we know so little about learning.

Human learning and, indeed, human intelligence begin to manifest themselves when children are several months old. At this point, children begin to explore themselves and their environments. They discover the existence of and the relationships between environmental stimuli and their own responses. In other terms, the children become aware of the association of the stimuli to which they have become conditioned and the responses which have been conditioned to the stimuli. They become aware of causes and effects in their worlds.

This awareness is a two-way street. For example, the child becomes aware that the nipple or the food serves as stimulus to a sucking or grasping response. This response, in turn, will lead to satisfying a need for nourishment. The child may also become aware that a need for nourishment stimulates the response of search for the nipple or the food.

In summary, through exploring, children become aware of both their past and present relationships to their environments—including themselves. Children attempt to describe where they are in relation to themselves and the worlds around them. **Exploring** is the first stage or phase of human learning. This form of exploration begins to distinguish humankind from all other forms of life.

It is a short step from becoming aware of the ingredients of human experience to anticipating experiences. With an increasing confidence in this awareness of the relationship of stimulus and response, the child is prepared for instrumental or purposeful learning at about one year of age. In other words, the child sets out to obtain a certain result or end, independent of the means to be employed. For example, the child may set out to attract its mother, or to obtain food or an object that is out of reach.

Drawing from this awareness of the relationship between stimulus and response or cause and effect, the child sets a goal of achieving certain effects. The goals of the instrumental act are often seen later although approximation of them was obviously intended from the beginning.

In summary, children understand their relationships to future events or experiences. They are, in effect, attempting to predict the consequences of their efforts. They understand where they want to be in their worlds. **Understanding** is the second stage or phase of human learning. It is what allows humankind to anticipate its future—another distinction from other forms of life.

The next phase of human learning flows naturally from the understanding phase. It involves the development of behavioral patterns instrumental to achieving goals. From the end of the first year onwards, the child draws from his or her repertoire of behaviors to produce the responses needed to achieve a goal. For example, the child may laugh or cry to bring the mother or surrogate to him or her. The child may move his or her hand in the direction of the unreachable food or object. There may be a series of trial-and-error experiences. These experiences may either confirm the child's responses, if the child reaches the goal and experiences satisfaction, or else they may reject the child's responses, if the child does not reach the goal.

In summary, children begin to act in order to get from where they are to where they want to be within their worlds. They are, in effect, attempting to control themselves and their worlds. **Acting** is the third stage or phase of learning. It enables human beings to plan and work toward the end of influencing their future.

The first year of human development serves as a prototype for all human learning. The child's reflexes are unknowingly conditioned as habitual responses to certain stimuli. These habits serve as the limited repertoire of responses with which the child initially approaches the world. Improvement in the quantity and quality of responses with which the learner ultimately relates to the world depends upon the development of the child's intelligence. This development of intelligence, in turn, depends upon how effectively he or she goes through the stages or phases of learning.

Initially, the child explores and identifies the nature of the stimuli and responses in his or her experience. Transitionally, the child comes to understand the interactive nature of stimuli and responses, anticipates the effects of one upon the other, and develops goals to achieve these effects. Finally, the child acts by drawing from his or her developing repertoire of responses to attempt to achieve goals. The child's action behavior is shaped by feedback or by the effect it achieves. This feedback recycles the stages or phases of learning as the child explores more extensively, understands more accurately, and acts more effectively. This ascending, enlarging spiral of exploration, understanding, and action is the source of the adult's improving repertoire of responses.

What goes on in the first year of life occurs in more and more refined ways throughout life. How effectively we live our lives depends totally upon how efficiently and effectively we learn.

Processing in Training

We can see the applications of human processing, both in and out of training. In the absence of education or training, people learn in naturalistic ways. In the presence of teaching or training, the teachers or trainers serve to facilitate the learners' or trainees' processing. Indeed, the central occurrence in the training delivery is the movement of the trainees through exploring the training experience, understanding the training goals, and acting upon the training programs.

Just watch people's exploratory activities in the absence of formal training. Personnel become interested in some object or mechanism on their own initiative at work. The personnel will approach the material or object and position themselves to give it their attention. They may observe the thing for a while, perhaps listen to it, and then probably touch it. The touching will lead to handling. If possible, personnel may try it out in different ways, turning the material around or over, or attaching it to other things.

The personnel may try to figure out what the thing is and does, and maybe even why and how it does it. Finally, they may try to do whatever it does. In the process, they have found out what they know about it, and what they can do with it. In short, they have found out where they are in relation to the learning experience. (So have their trainers, if they are present.)

In training, the trainees must address all sources of learning in a similar manner. If the trainer is presenting some content, the trainees must use all of their exploring skills to address the trainer, the content, the delivery or method, and the immediate environment as dimensions of the training experience. Trainees must also address themselves as potential sources of learning, in terms of the learning experiences and learning skills that they bring to the learning process. By exploring all dimensions of the training experience, the trainees can find out where they are in relation to the training experience. They will be ready to find out where they want to be.

The trainees may then engage in a series of understanding activities. They may relate the dimensions of their current training experiences to those of their past experiences. They may organize the dimensions of these experiences in different ways based upon their similarities and differences. The trainees may organize the dimensions of the training experience in still different ways based upon their functions and the values of these functions to their learning. The trainees may generalize their needs from these values, and set generalized training goals based upon the training experience and specific training objectives derived from the different dimensions of the training experience. Or they may do all of this by simply determining what, of all the content possible, they have yet to learn.

Where there is a trainer with a training goal, all of these activities can take place in relation to the training goal. The trainees may set their training objectives in relation to the training goals. Where there is no trainer, the trainees may set their learning objectives based upon their generalized needs. In summary, the trainees gain increasing confidence in their understanding of where they are in relation to where they want to be. They are ready to act in order to get there.

Observing the trainees in the action phase reveals the types of activities in which trainees engage. First, they work to master the knowledge and skills involved in the training goals. If the trainers have established the goal, the trainees learn the knowledge or skills the trainers have developed. If trainers are not involved, people begin to define their skills objectives in terms of the deficits or problems they are having in achieving their goals, and to develop and implement programs designed to achieve those objectives.

In either event, having acquired the learning, the trainees can repeat or practice the skill involved until it is ready and effectively available to them. Then they can apply the skills, either in some way that was intended by the trainer or in a way that is relevant to their own experience. The trainees can continue to apply it in real-life, everyday living, learning, playing, and working experiences. Finally, they can transfer the learning to unique and creative situations in their lives. The culmination of mastery is to be able to create with what you have learned.

The training voyage, then, begins where the trainees are. Before our trainees can embark upon their training journeys, they must be able to identify the degrees of longitude and latitude at their points of origin. In terms of the training process, they must know precisely where they are in relation to the training experience. In order to know this, they first must explore where they are. Trainee exploration is the first phase of training.

PHASES OF TRAINING
I
EXPLORING
Where They Are

When the trainees know where they are, then they can determine their ports of destination. They must know the degrees of longitude and latitude of their objectives. In terms of the training process, the trainees must understand where they are in relation to where they want to be, and also what they will need to obtain from the training experience in order to get there. Trainee understanding is the second phase of training.

PHASES OF TRAINING

I		II
EXPLORING	⟶	UNDERSTANDING
Where They Are		Where They Want To Be

Finally, when the trainees have established their ports of destination clearly in mind, they can begin their training voyages. When they understand where they are in relation to where they want to be, they can act in order to get there. In other words, trainees can develop their own individualized learning processes, designed to achieve their training objectives. Trainee acting is the third phase of training.

PHASES OF TRAINING

I		II		III
EXPLORING	⟶	UNDERSTANDING	⟶	ACTING
Where They Are		Where They Want To Be		To Get There

All productive training is recycled. The trainees receive feedback from acting. The feedback stimulates more extensive exploration, more accurate understanding, and more effective action. The recycling intensifies the training experience. For healthy and growing people, it continues throughout life in an upwardly expanding spiral of learning.

PHASES OF TRAINING

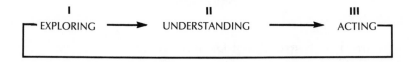

I		II		III
EXPLORING	⟶	UNDERSTANDING	⟶	ACTING

Everything the trainer does must directly facilitate the trainees' movement through the training process. At all stages of training, the trainer must be guided by what is effective for the trainees. In the end, the trainer's effectiveness will be determined by his or her ability to facilitate the trainees' recycling of training in a life-long learning process. How the training skills relate directly to the trainees' movement through the training or learning process is the exciting topic of *Making the Training Delivery*, Book II of *Training Delivery Skills*.

Overview

In Book I, we concentrated upon preparing the training delivery (see Figure 1-1). In terms of the training design,

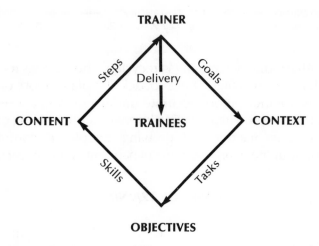

Figure **1-1.** Instructional Design

the emphasis was on defining the training skill objectives, developing the skill content, and developing the delivery plan. In other words, after establishing the productivity goals and analyzing the contextual tasks, the tasks of the training design were initiated (Carkhuff, 1983a; Carkhuff, Fisher, Cannon, Friel and Pierce, 1984).

Now we are going to make the training delivery to the trainees. To insure that the trainees receive the delivery, we will learn several sets of training skills. Then we will assess the effectiveness of the training delivery (see Figure 1-2) by evaluating the following: training-learning process, acquisition of skill content, application to skill objective, transfer to contextual tasks, and achievement of productivity goals.

INSTRUCTIONAL EVALUATION

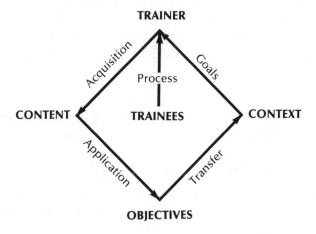

Figure 1-2. Instructional Evaluation

We can get a preview of the training skills of this volume by looking at the training delivery processes (see Figure 1-3). As can be seen, the training delivery skills (*TDS*) to be learned will serve to facilitate the trainees' movement through exploring, understanding, and acting. Thus, the content processing skills (*CPS*) to be filled in relate the content to the trainees: *CPS* enable us to teach content. In turn, the interpersonal processing skills (*IPS*) to be filled in relate the trainees to the content and the trainer: *IPS* enable us to teach trainees. Together, the *CPS* and *IPS* converge to comprise the training management skills (*TMS*) that enable us to implement the training delivery plan.

As can be seen, the training delivery plan is the culmination of preparing the training content. While extensive, this planning occurs during the pre-training phase of training. All of the preparatory effort occurs prior to involving the trainees in training. Preparing the training content is a necessary but not sufficient condition of making a training delivery. It remains for us to learn the training delivery skills that implement the training delivery plan. The training delivery skills will make us productive trainers in the Age of Information. Making a training delivery is the topic of this volume.

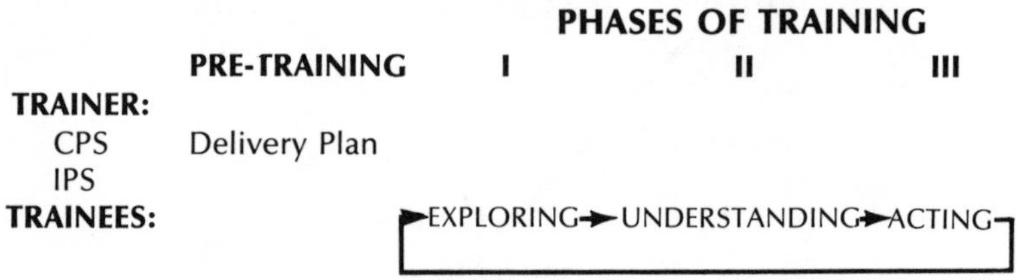

PHASES OF TRAINING

	PRE-TRAINING	I	II	III
TRAINER:				
CPS	Delivery Plan			
IPS				
TRAINEES:		►EXPLORING► UNDERSTANDING►ACTING┐		

CPS—Content Processing Skills
IPS —Interpersonal Processing Skills

Figure 1-3. The Training Process Skills Facilitating Trainee Processing

References

Ausebel, D.; Novak, J.; and Havesian, H. *Educational Psychology*. New York: Holt, Rinehart and Winston, 1978.

Bloom, B. S. *Mastery Learning: Theory and Practice*. New York: Holt, Rinehart and Winston, 1971.

Carkhuff, R. R. *Sources of Human Productivity*. Amherst, Mass.: Human Resource Development Press, 1983.(a)

Carkhuff, R. R. *Interpersonal Skills and Human Productivity*. Amherst, Mass.: Human Resource Development Press, 1983.(b)

Carkhuff, R. R.; and Pierce, R. M. *Training Delivery Skills: I. Preparing the Training Delivery*. Amherst, Mass.: Human Resource Development Press, 1984.

Carkhuff, R.R.; Fisher, S.G.; Cannon, J.R.; Friel, T.W. and Pierce, R.M. *Instructional Systems Design, Volumes I and II*. Amherst, Mass.: Human Resource Development Press, 1984.

Dewey, J. *How We Think*. Boston: D.C. Heath, 1910.

Gagne, R. M. *Conditions of Learning*. New York: Holt, Rinehart and Winston, 1977.

Guilford, J. P. *The Nature of Human Intelligence*. New York: McGraw-Hill, 1967.

Piaget, J. *The Psychology of Intelligence*. London: Routledge and Kegan Paul, 1950.

Piaget, J. *The Origins of Intelligence in Children*. New York: International Universities Press, 1952.

Piaget, J.; and Inhelder, B. *The Psychology of the Child*. New York: Basic Books, 1969.

2

Training Delivery Skills: An Overview

M aking the training delivery is the critical source of effectiveness in training. Until now, we have done nothing but prepare for making the training delivery (Carkhuff and Pierce, 1984). In other words, we have not yet accounted for one percent of training effectiveness. We have, to be sure, prepared our training delivery. This preparation is a necessary but not sufficient condition of training. It remains for us to make the training delivery. Making the training delivery emphasizes facilitating the trainees' movement through exploration, understanding, and acting (Carkhuff, 1983; Carkhuff, Fisher, Cannon, Friel and Pierce, 1984).

Again, training delivery skills are best conceived as part of the larger instructional intervention. The training skill objectives have been defined, the skill content developed, and the delivery plan organized. Training delivery skills emphasize the skills involved in making the training delivery.

The training skill objective of this book is as follows:

The instructional trainees will be able to make the training delivery by implementing training delivery skills under formal and informal work conditions at levels that insure trainee application and transfer.

Before you learn to identify and perform training delivery skills, you may want an index of your present level of understanding. Take some time to outline the critical tasks of making a training delivery.

_____

_____

_____

_____

_____

Indexing Training Delivery Skills

You did very well if you emphasized both the content and the trainer functions of making a training delivery. Trainers teach content. Trainers teach trainees. Together, the following training delivery skills facilitate making a productive training delivery which, in turn, can be evaluated by training evaluation skills:

Content Processing Skills:	Processing training content
Interpersonal Processing Skills:	Processing trainees' experiences
Training Management Skills:	Processing trainees through the delivery plan
Training Evaluation Skills:	Evaluating training processes and outcomes

Listed above are the training delivery skills presented in this volume. They are, to be sure, dependent upon the training preparation skills of Book I.

Overviewing Training Delivery Skills

Preparing the Training Delivery

Preparing the training delivery involves developing the training content and organizing the training delivery plan. All of this occurs before the trainer has made contact with the trainees. In other words, the training delivery plan is developed in the pre-training phase of training. How we implement our training delivery plan will determine how effective our training is.

PHASES OF TRAINING

PRE-TRAINING

TRAINER:

    CPS   Delivery Plan

    IPS

TRAINEES:

Developing the training content emphasizes defining the training skill objective and developing the skill content to achieve it. The skill objective is defined in terms of its components, functions, processes, conditions, and standards. The skill content is developed in terms of the skill steps and supportive knowledge needed to achieve the training skill objective.

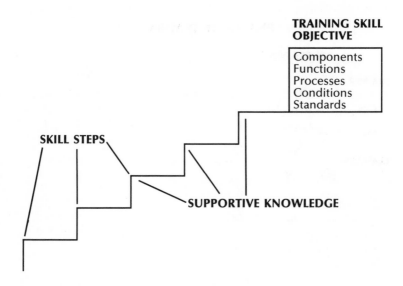

TRAINING SKILL OBJECTIVE

Components
Functions
Processes
Conditions
Standards

SKILL STEPS

SUPPORTIVE KNOWLEDGE

Developing the Training Content

Developing the training delivery plan emphasizes organizing the content and training methods. The content is organized to include the following: *reviewing* the trainees' contingency skills, *overviewing* the skill applications, *presenting* and *exercising* the skill steps, and *summarizing* the trainees' skill performances. The training methods are organized around a variety of media for *telling, showing,* and *doing.* It is important to view the training delivery plan in terms of its emphasis upon trainer and trainee or learner performance. As can be seen, the great majority of the training effort should be invested in managing trainee learning. Thus, learner or trainee management dominates the Review, Exercise, and Summary. Trainer and trainees share the responsibility for the Overview. During the Presentation, the trainer *tells* and *shows* so that the trainees or learners can *do* or perform the skills or skill steps involved.

CONTENT ORGANIZATION

TRAINING METHODS	Review Contingency Skills	Overview Skill Applications	Present Skill Steps	Exercise Skill Steps	Summarize Skill Performance
Tell	L	T & L	T	L	L
Show	L	T & L	T	L	L
Do	L	T & L	L	L	L

L = Learner
T = Trainer

Managing Trainee Learning

Making the Training Delivery

Making the training delivery emphasizes processing the training delivery plan. In other words, armed with the delivery plan, the trainer facilitates the training process, emphasizing trainee exploring, understanding, and acting. The trainer uses content processing skills *(CPS)* and interpersonal processing skills *(IPS)* in implementing the delivery plan. For example, while the trainees are reviewing their contingency skills, the trainers are using their training delivery skills to facilitate trainee processing.

PHASES OF TRAINING

	PRE-TRAINING	I	II	III
TRAINER:				
CPS	Delivery Plan			
IPS				
TRAINEES:	►EXPLORING►UNDERSTANDING ► ACTING			

Content processing skills *(CPS)* emphasize processing trainee learning based upon the content of the training delivery plan. Thus, we diagnose the trainees' levels of functioning in relation to the content. Based upon the diagnoses, we set training goals. Finally, based upon the goals, we develop training programs to achieve the goals. In other words, we teach the content by seeing the trainees through the eyes of the content.

PHASES OF TRAINING

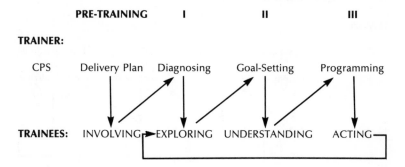

Content Processing Skills

Interpersonal processing skills *(IPS)* emphasize processing the content based upon the trainee's experience. Thus, we respond to the trainee's experience of the training content, personalize the trainee's experience of the training goals and individualize the trainee's experience of the training programs. In other words, we teach the trainees by seeing the content through their eyes.

PHASES OF TRAINING

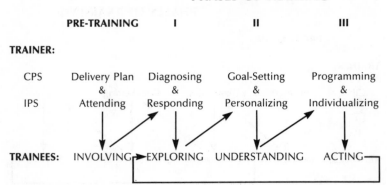

	PRE-TRAINING	I	II	III
TRAINER:				
CPS	Delivery Plan	Diagnosing	Goal-Setting	Programming
	&	&	&	&
IPS	Attending	Responding	Personalizing	Individualizing
TRAINEES:	INVOLVING	EXPLORING	UNDERSTANDING	ACTING

Interpersonal Processing Skills

The *CPS* and *IPS* occur simultaneously in the implementation of the training delivery plan. Together, the *CPS* and *IPS* comprise the training management skills which implement the delivery plan. Each serves to complement the other in facilitating the trainees' processing. Thus, the trainer's diagnosing and responding facilitate trainee exploring. The trainer's goal-setting and personalizing facilitate trainee understanding. The trainer's programming and individualizing facilitate trainee acting. The *CPS* operate in the terms of the external frame of reference of the content. The *IPS* function in terms of the internal frames of reference of the trainees.

Training Management Skills

Thus, in the pre-training phase, the trainer develops the training delivery plan and attends to the trainees. In developing the training delivery plan, the trainer attends to the trainees in their absence. In other words, the trainer develops the delivery plan with an emphasis upon managing trainee learning. In the presence of the trainees, the trainer attends to them directly by attending physically, observing, and listening to them. The trainer does so in order to involve the trainees in the training process. Developing the training delivery plan is the topic of Chapter 9, Book I, *Preparing the Training Delivery.*

PRE-TRAINING

TRAINER:

CPS   Delivery Plan
                   &
IPS   Attending

TRAINEES: INVOLVING

Pre-Training: Developing the Training Delivery Plan

In Phase I of training, the trainer works with the trainees to diagnose their performance and respond to their experiences. He or she diagnoses the trainees from the external frames of reference of their levels of functioning on the content. The trainer responds to the trainees from their own internal frames of reference of their experiences of the content. Together, diagnosing and responding facilitate the trainees' exploring where they are in relation to the training experience. Diagnosing and responding are the topics of Chapters 3, 4, and 5 of this volume.

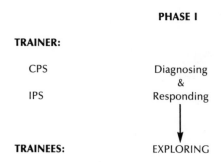

Phase I: Diagnosing and Responding

In Phase II of training, the trainer works with the trainees to set and personalize training goals. They set training goals based upon the contextual content diagnoses. The trainer works with the trainees to personalize the training goals based upon the trainees' internal experiences. Together, the goal-setting and personalizing facilitate the trainees' understanding of where they want to be in relation to the training experience. Goal-setting and personalizing are the topics of Chapters 3, 4, and 5 of this volume.

PHASE II

TRAINER:

CPS	Goal-Setting
	&
IPS	Personalizing

TRAINEES: UNDERSTANDING

Phase II: Goal-Setting and Personalizing

In Phase III of training, the trainer works with the trainees to develop and individualize training programs. The trainers develop programs to achieve the external training goals they have set. The trainer works with the trainees to individualize the programs based upon the trainees' internal experiences. Together, programming and individualizing facilitate the trainees' acting to achieve their training goals. Programming and individualizing are the topics of Chapters 3, 4, and 5 of this volume.

PHASE III

TRAINER:

CPS

Programming

&

IPS

Individualizing

TRAINEES:

ACTING

Phase III: Programming and Individualizing

In addition to the phases previously depicted, there is a post-training phase. During the post-training phase the trainer works with the trainees to recycle the phases of training based upon the feedback the trainees have received from acting. In other words, the trainees receive feedback on their skill performance. The trainers work with the trainees to monitor the external performance feedback and respond to the trainees' internal experiences. Together, monitoring and responding serve to stimulate recycling the training process: more extensive exploring; more accurate understanding; more effective acting. Monitoring and responding are the topics of Chapters 3 and 4 of this volume.

POST-TRAINING

TRAINER:

CPS

IPS

Monitoring
&
Responding

↓

TRAINEES:

RECYCLING

Post-Training: Recycling the Phases of Training

It is important to emphasize that the training delivery process occurs within the implementation of the training delivery plan. Again, the training delivery plan emphasizes managing trainee learning. Within the training delivery plan, the trainer focuses upon facilitating trainee processing: exploring, understanding, and acting. Indeed, there may be many individual as well as group recyclings of this processing. Basically, the trainees' processing enables them to act to receive the training content. The feedback to the acting serves to facilitate spiraling trainee experience and performance.

References

Carkhuff, R. R. *Sources of Human Productivity*. Amherst, Mass.: Human Resource Development Press, 1983.

Carkhuff, R.R., Fisher, S.G., Cannon, J.R., Friel, T.W. and Pierce, R.M. *Instructional Systems Design, Volumes I and II*. Amherst, Mass.: Human Resource Development Press, 1984.

Carkhuff, R. R. and Pierce, R. M. *Training Delivery Skills: I. Preparing the Training Delivery*. Amherst, Mass.: Human Resource Development Press, 1984.

II

TRAINING DELIVERY SKILLS

*T*raining delivery skills (TDS) are those skills involved in delivering the training content. TDS are used in implementing the training delivery plan. They emphasize content processing skills (CPS) and interpersonal processing skills (IPS). CPS process the trainees through the requirements of the content. IPS process the content through the experiences of the trainees. Together, CPS and IPS facilitate the trainees' exploring, understanding, and acting upon the training content. When utilized simultaneously in implementing the training delivery plan, CPS and IPS define training management skills.

PHASES OF TRAINING

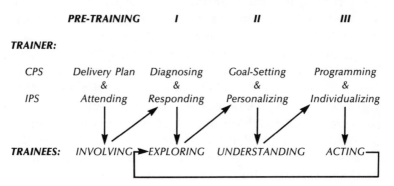

3

Content Processing Skills

Most trainers think of training in terms of the content when they think of making the training delivery. Productivity goals were individualized to become unit goals. Contextual tasks were analyzed to achieve the unit goals. The skills that comprised the tasks were defined as training skill objectives. The skill steps and knowledge content were developed to achieve the skills. The training delivery plan was designed. Now all that remains is to implement the delivery plan, making the delivery of the content to the trainees. Right? Wrong! The trainers must use a special set of skills to make the delivery of the content within the implementation of the delivery plan. Later on, we will see that the trainers will need another set of skills to relate the trainees to the content. In making the training delivery, the trainers funnel their content, organization, and methods into the training process in which they involve their trainees. Again, the training process involves the trainees in *exploring* where they are with the content, *understanding* where they want or need to be, and *acting* to get to their training goals. Training delivery skills facilitate the trainees' movement through these phases of training.

The delivery of any content in any area of human endeavor requires both an external and an internal emphasis (Carkhuff and Berenson, 1981; O'Neill and Spielburger, 1978). The external emphasis represents the content to be delivered. It is based upon the recipients' movement through levels of skill development (Berenson, Berenson and Carkhuff, 1979). At each step of the skill development process, the recipients' progress is assessed. Trainers are facilitative in delivering their content when they: 1) diagnose the trainees in terms of their needs (Cornwell, 1981; Nadler, 1982; Pfeiffer, 1966); 2) select and specify goals that are congruent with trainees' needs (Flanders, 1960, 1963; Hills, 1981; Miller and Rose, 1979; Ribler, 1983); 3) present the material in a highly cognitive and atomistic manner (Kaya, Gerhard, Staslewski, and Berenson, 1967); and then 4) monitor the training in terms of the goals that were specified (Campbell, 1977; Clark, 1971; Gagne, 1977; Gilbert, 1978; Hudgins, 1974; Mager and Beach, 1966). All of these functions are incorporated in content processing skills *(CPS)*.

Principles of Content Processing

CARNEGIE LIBRARY
LIVINGSTONE COLLEGE
SALISBURY, N. C. 28144

Our content processing skills *(CPS)* training objective in this lesson is as follows:

> *The instructional trainees will make training deliveries by implementing content processing skills under formal and informal conditions at levels that facilitate their trainees' process movement.*

Before you learn content processing skills, you may want an index of your skills in this area. Perhaps you can take a training skill objective in your specialty content and outline the training delivery content processing you would use to facilitate achievement of this objective.

_____

_____

_____

_____

_____

Indexing Content Processing Skills

You should be pleased if you emphasized delivering the content to the trainees. These *CPS* will include diagnosing the trainees in terms of the content, setting goals based upon the diagnosis, programming based upon the goals, and monitoring based upon the programs.

> **DIAGNOSING:** Diagnosing trainees' levels of functioning on content in order to facilitate trainee exploration.
>
> **SETTING GOALS:** Setting goals for skills and knowledge based upon the diagnosis in order to facilitate trainee understanding.
>
> **PROGRAMMING:** Developing steps to achieve goals in order to facilitate trainee acting.
>
> **MONITORING:** Observing feedback from acting in order to facilitate trainee recycling of the training process.

PHASES OF TRAINING

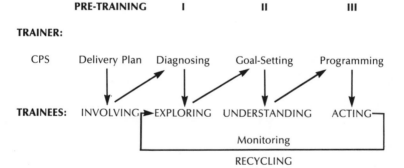

Overviewing Content Processing Skills

Preparing Delivery Plans

We have already attended to training delivery planning skills in Book I. We have developed our content, planned our deliveries and training methods, and developed our training delivery plans before coming into contact with the trainees. In other words, preparing the delivery plan takes place before learning ensues. The relationship between the prepared delivery plan and the phases of the training delivery is important to understand. The exploring-understanding-acting (E-U-A) training process is an ongoing one. In making the training delivery, the E-U-A process is recycled for every stage of the delivery plan. Thus, the trainer is constantly diagnosing, setting goals, programming, and monitoring in order to facilitate the trainees' E-U-A process.

Planning Delivery

Within every stage of the training delivery plan, the trainer facilitates the trainees' E-U-A. For example, within the Review of the trainees' contingency skills, the trainer is using content processing skills to facilitate the trainees' E-U-A: diagnosing the trainees' functioning; setting goals based upon the diagnosis; developing programs based upon the goals; and monitoring the programs. Content processing skills emphasize moment-to-moment programming for training achievement. *CPS* make the learning process live. *CPS* make the delivery plan work.

CONTENT ORGANIZATION

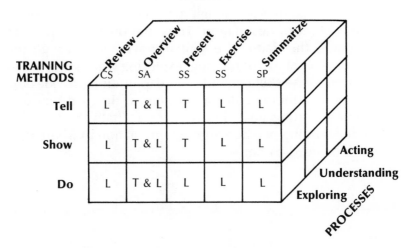

CS = Contingency Skills   SP = Skill Performance
SA = Skill Applications   L = Learner
SS = Skill Steps   T = Trainer

Managing Content Processing

Diagnosing Trainees

Diagnosing the trainees is where the training delivery begins. The diagnosis lets us know where the trainees are functioning in terms of the skill content. It also lets the trainees know where they are beginning their training experience. By letting both trainer and trainees know the point of the trainees' entry into the training experience, the diagnosis allows them to detail the training goals and programs. Most important, it allows both trainer and trainees to tailor the learning of the content to the trainees' unique needs. In other words, an accurate diagnosis is the basis for individualizing the training process in terms of the trainees' abilities to perform the skills content. In short, the diagnosis tells us the degrees of latitude and longitude from which the individual trainees embark upon their training journey. It enables us to determine precisely the degrees of latitude and longitude which we seek to achieve at our point of destination. Thus, the diagnostic process facilitates the trainees' essential movement through the exploration phase of training: exploring where they are in relation to the skill content. This exploration provides the necessary conditions for movement to the next phase of training: setting goals in order to facilitate the trainees' understanding of where they are in relation to where they want or need to be.

Diagnosing

The essential question in diagnosis is: Can the individual trainees perform the skill? The answer to this question enables us to make a functional diagnosis. If the trainees can perform the skill, then they are ready to learn the next skill. If the trainees cannot perform the skill, then we must diagnose the skill steps they *can* perform. For example, when training personnel to schedule tasks, we begin our diagnosis by asking if the trainees can perform the first step: Can trainees identify job tasks? If the trainees are able to identify job tasks, then they are ready to learn the skills involved in ordering the job tasks. If the trainees cannot identify the job tasks, then we must further diagnose the trainees' performances on the skill substeps underlying this skill step.

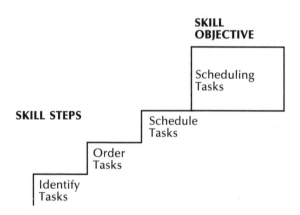

Diagnosing Skill and Skill Steps

Thus, if the trainees cannot perform the skill step, then we must discriminate the things they can do from those they cannot do. After identifying a deficit in skill step performance, we diagnose skill substep performance. In other words, we must determine the substeps which the trainee can perform on the way to achievement of the skill step. For example, if our trainees could not identify the job tasks, we diagnose the individual substeps each trainee can or cannot perform leading up to the identifying tasks skill step. The level at which the trainees perform the skill substep dictates where we set the next skill objective.

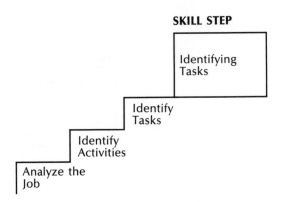

SKILL STEP

Identifying Tasks

Identify Tasks

Identify Activities

Analyze the Job

Diagnosing Skill Substeps

If the trainees cannot perform a given skill substep, it may be because they lack the supportive knowledge. The next stage of diagnosing the trainees involves a diagnosis of their level of supportive knowledge. The trainees may lack the facts which involve the components and functions of the skill substeps, or the concepts which involve the various causal or correlational relationships between and among the components and functions. The trainees may lack the principles which state not only the various relationships but also their implications, such as the benefits that are derived from these relationships. For example, in training the job task analysis substep we may teach the principle of input and output: if the inputs and outputs are identified for each worker behavior, then all the tasks can be identified so that the work flow can be scheduled correctly.

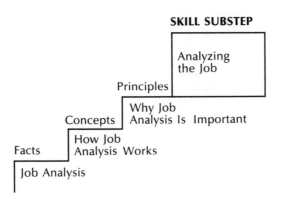

Diagnosing Supportive Knowledge

The diagnosis should describe the trainees' levels of functioning with regard to the skill steps and skill substeps as well as the supportive knowledge. Both trainees and trainer should have an observable index of the trainees' performances. This enables both to know the point of entry into the training experience. At this point, select a training skill objective for which you have developed your delivery plan and training methods. Develop your skill steps, skill substeps, and supportive knowledge so that you can diagnose your trainees' levels of functioning.

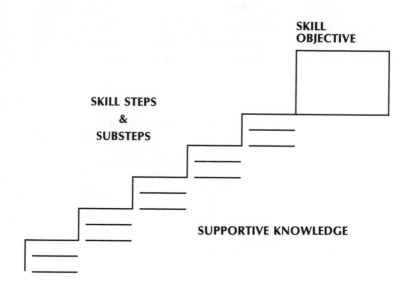

Practicing Diagnosing

Setting Training Goals

The purpose of the diagnosis is to set goals for the trainees. The diagnosis lets us know where the trainees are functioning in terms of the skills content. Goal-setting lets us know where the trainees will learn to function. Our goal-setting skills enable us to define in detail the trainees' goals and objectives. The goals and objectives are within the grasp of the trainees because they are based upon accurate diagnoses of the trainees. Most important, goal-setting enables both trainer and trainees to translate the established training skill objectives into goals that are tailored to the trainees' unique needs. Again, the point of origin as well as the destination of the training experience is known to the trainees due to the trainer's diagnostic and goal-setting skills. The unique needs of the trainees can be met in their special training programs. Thus, our goal-setting process facilitates the trainees' essential movement through the understanding phase of training: understanding where they are in relation to where they want or need to be with the skill content. This understanding provides the necessary conditions for movement to the next phase of training: developing programs in order to facilitate the trainees' action programs, to get them from where they are to where they want or need to be with the skills content.

Training Goals

The essential question of goal-setting is: What skills will the trainees be able to perform? Obviously, the answer is based upon the skill diagnosis. Diagnosis of the trainees' ability to perform the skill will determine the next level of skill step objectives. For example, if the trainees can identify job tasks, then ordering job tasks becomes the next skill step objective.

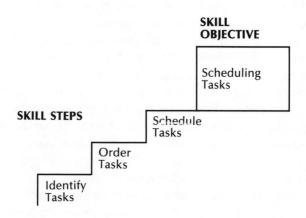

Setting Skill Step Objectives

After we have established a skill step objective, then we determine the level of skill substep performance that the trainees will learn. For example, if we are teaching the skill step of identifying tasks, we may set a substep objective of analyzing the job process for trainees who we diagnose as being unable to perform that skill substep. Again, the level at which the trainees perform the skill substep dictates where we set the next skill step objective.

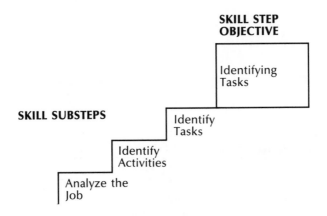

SKILL STEP OBJECTIVE

Identifying Tasks

SKILL SUBSTEPS

Identify Tasks

Identify Activities

Analyze the Job

Setting Skill Substep Objectives

If the trainees cannot perform a given skill substep because they lack the supportive knowledge, then we must set objectives for learning the supportive knowledge. For example, if the trainees lack comprehension of the principle of identifying inputs and outputs in job analysis, then this principle becomes the supportive knowledge objective: if the inputs and outputs are identified for each worker behavior, then all the tasks can be identified so that work flow can be scheduled correctly.

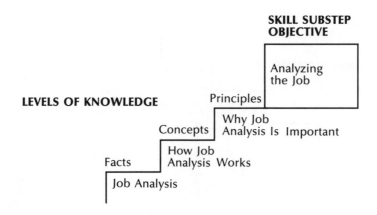

SKILL SUBSTEP OBJECTIVE

Analyzing the Job

LEVELS OF KNOWLEDGE

Principles

Concepts — Why Job Analysis Is Important

Facts — How Job Analysis Works

Job Analysis

Setting Supportive Knowledge Objectives

Goal-setting should define the trainees' target levels of functioning for skills and knowledge. Both trainees and trainer must have observable goals and objectives that both will know have been achieved. Thus, both will be able to identify the point of exit from the training experience.

At this point, again use a training skill objective for which you have developed your delivery plan and training methods. Develop objectives for skill steps, skill substeps, and supportive knowledge depending upon your diagnosis of the trainees' levels of functioning.

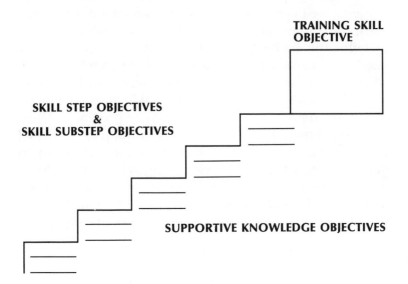

TRAINING SKILL OBJECTIVE

SKILL STEP OBJECTIVES
&
SKILL SUBSTEP OBJECTIVES

SUPPORTIVE KNOWLEDGE OBJECTIVES

Practicing Goal-Setting Skills

Developing Training Programs

The purpose of the training program is to help the trainees achieve the training goals. Our diagnostic skills showed us where the trainees are functioning. Our goal-setting skills showed us where the trainees will learn to function. Now, our program development or programming skills show us how the trainees will get there. Our programming skills enable us to develop and implement the steps leading toward the achievement of our objectives. Each skill step and skill substep objective is broken down to an atomistic level, beginning with our trainees' levels of functioning. This way, we insure that our trainees can achieve the objectives. Most important, our programming skills enable us to tailor the training programs to the trainees' unique needs. Again, the trainees know where they are beginning, where they are going, and how to get there. They have every assurance that they will achieve their objectives, due to the systematic development of their training programs. Thus, our programming skills facilitate the trainees' essential movement through the action phase of training: acting to get from where they are to where they want or need to be with the skill content. The trainees can act to achieve their training goals, and they can learn from the effectiveness of their actions how to modify future training programs.

Training Programs

The essential question of programming is: Can we break down the skills to the objective so that the trainees can perform them? In planning the skill content, we used programming skills to identify skill steps, skill substeps, and supportive knowledge. We now recycle the content development process based upon our diagnoses of the trainees' performances and the newly established objective. For example, when the trainees can identify job tasks, then they can learn the next programmatic step contributing to the overall skill objective of scheduling tasks. If needed, the skill steps identified during the content development stage may be modified within each trainee's individual training program. We will learn more about individualizing content in a later section of this book.

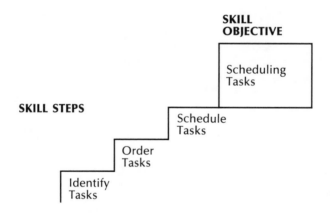

SKILL OBJECTIVE

Scheduling Tasks

SKILL STEPS

Schedule Tasks

Order Tasks

Identify Tasks

Developing the Skill Step Program

After we have developed the skill step program, we must develop the skill substeps to achieve each step. For example, when training personnel in task scheduling, we may set a skill step objective of identifying the job tasks. Next, we will develop the substeps to performing the skill step: analyzing the job, identifying the activities, and identifying the tasks.

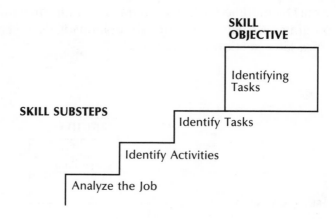

SKILL OBJECTIVE

Identifying Tasks

SKILL SUBSTEPS

Identify Tasks

Identify Activities

Analyze the Job

Developing the Skill Substep Program

Upon the development of the skill substeps, we may discover that there are certain facts and/or concepts and/or principles that the trainees lack. For example, the trainees may lack the factual knowledge of what a job analysis is: a job analysis is a methodology for identifying the components, processes, and functions of a particular job. The needed supportive knowledge is developed and added to the training program.

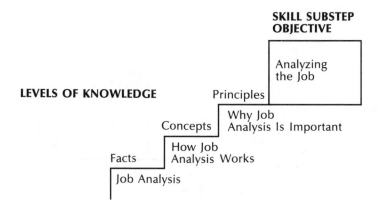

Developing the Supportive Knowledge Program

Our programming develops the skill steps, skill sub-steps, and supportive knowledge which the trainees require in order to achieve the training skill objective. Based upon the diagnosis of the trainees' levels of functioning, the training program provides all of the skills and knowledge required to achieve the training skill objective. The trainees have atomistic programs that lead them to their training goals. At this point, refer again to the training skill objective for which you have developed your training delivery plan. Develop the skill steps, skill substeps and supportive knowledge for your trainees based upon their unique training objectives.

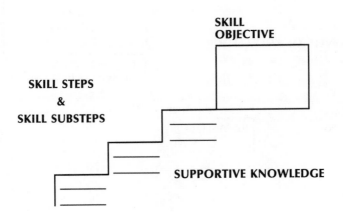

SKILL OBJECTIVE

SKILL STEPS & SKILL SUBSTEPS

SUPPORTIVE KNOWLEDGE

Practicing Programming

Monitoring Trainee Performance

The purpose of the monitoring program is to observe the feedback resulting from the trainees' performances. Once the trainees have acted on their programs to achieve the training skill objective, they receive feedback from their actions. The purpose of the monitoring is to assess this feedback. The monitoring skills enable us to assess the applications the trainees have made using the skills they have supposedly acquired. In other words, the monitoring skills assess the skills application under real-life conditions. That, after all, is what the training process is all about. Our trainees have acted upon their training programs. They are attempting to apply the skills they have acquired. Monitoring skills will allow us to assess the effectiveness of this application. Accordingly, the most effective times for the trainer to use the monitoring skills will be during the Exercise and Summary experiences. In so doing, our monitoring skills will serve to facilitate a recycling of training. The trainees have acted by attempting to perform the skill, and will now receive feedback from their actions. This feedback will serve to stimulate more extensive exploration of where the trainees now are in relation to training; they will thus obtain a more accurate understanding of where they now want or need to be, and therefore be able to determine more effective action to help them learn to perform the skill correctly.

Monitoring

The first application of monitoring is monitoring skill step performance. The discrimination to be made is simply whether or not the trainees have applied the skill steps. If the skill step has been performed, then the trainee is giving evidence of readiness for the next training experience. If the skill step has not been performed, then the trainee must recycle the current training experience. For example, monitoring will determine whether or not the trainee has identified the job tasks. This recycling process may require new training goals to be set and new programming to be done, in order to achieve the skill step objective.

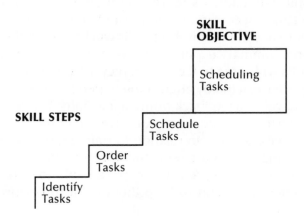

Monitoring Skill Step Performance

The second use of monitoring is when we apply this technique to the performance of skill substeps. If the skill step has not been performed, then the training process must be recycled at the skill substep level. For example, the trainee may be able to analyze the job but unable to identify job activities. This new diagnosis facilitates the trainee's expanded exploration of where he or she is in terms of skill step performance. The recycling process may require that a new skill substep objective be set, i.e., identifying job activities. A new program may need to be developed to initiate more effective action toward the achievement of this skill substep objective.

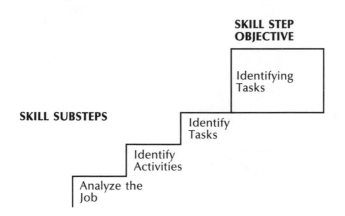

Monitoring Skill Substep Performance

The third use of monitoring is checking the level of supportive knowledge available to the trainee. If a skill sub-step cannot be performed, then the supportive knowledge must be assessed in a recycling of the training process. For example, if the trainee cannot identify job activities, it may be because the trainee lacks some level of supportive knowledge. Perhaps the trainee cannot comprehend one or more of the facts, concepts, and principles. This knowledge becomes an objective, and a training program is developed to achieve the objective.

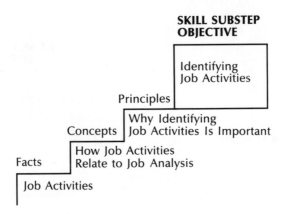

SKILL SUBSTEP OBJECTIVE

Identifying Job Activities

Principles

Why Identifying Job Activities Is Important

Concepts

How Job Activities Relate to Job Analysis

Facts

Job Activities

Monitoring Supportive Knowledge

Our monitoring skills enable us to assess the performance of skills and to recycle the training into a new training experience or to recycle the trainee through select dimensions of the same or similar training experience. If the trainee fails to transfer the skill correctly, then the training process is recycled. The levels of skill steps, skill substeps, and supportive knowledge are diagnosed in order to help the trainee explore where he or she wants or needs to be. Programs are developed to help the trainee get there. At this point, use a training skill objective for which you have developed your delivery plan. Make certain you are prepared to monitor the skill transfer in order to determine whether to cycle the trainee into a new training experience, or recycle the trainee through the same training experience. Identify the skill steps, skill substeps, and supportive knowledge to be monitored.

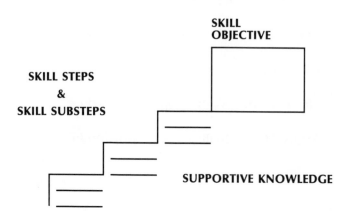

Practicing Monitoring

Exercising

Again, we employ our training delivery skills to facilitate the trainees' movement through E-U-A. We can use our *CPS* for making training deliveries when "thinking on our feet," in or out of the classroom. We can apply the *CPS* skills in any critical situation that involves training and learning. For example, not only can we use them in communicating with superiors or subordinates at work, we can also use our *CPS* in communicating at home with our spouses or friends. We could also train our trainees in the basic *CPS* skills so that they would be able to diagnose, set goals, program, and monitor their own performance.

SKILL OBJECTIVE:

Trainees will discriminate levels of performance within the work setting by learning content processing skills so that levels of process movement can be identified and work content achieved.

DIAGNOSE: Skills, steps, knowledge

SET GOALS: Skills, steps, knowledge

PROGRAM: Skills, steps, knowledge

MONITOR: Skills, steps, knowledge

Exercising Content Processing Skills

You may wish to do a repeat exercise using your content processing skills. Again, use a selected training skill objective. Develop your diagnoses, goals, programs, and monitoring plan.

SKILL OBJECTIVE:

_____

_____

_____

DIAGNOSE: _____

_____

SET GOALS: _____

_____

PROGRAM: _____

_____

MONITOR: _____

_____

Exercising Content Processing Skills

Describe how you might apply your content processing skills within a living or home setting, a learning or training setting, and a working or job setting. Try to identify as many applications as possible.

LIVING: _____

_____

_____

LEARNING: _____

_____

_____

WORKING: _____

_____

_____

Applying Content Processing Skills

Summarizing

Perhaps you can now outline your content processing skills for training in your specialty skill content. Simply outline the content processing by which you would facilitate the achievement of your training skill objective.

_____

_____

_____

_____

_____

If you are able to outline your content processing skills, then we are pleased because we have accomplished our training skill objective:

> *The instructional trainees will make training deliveries by implementing content processing skills under formal and informal conditions at levels that facilitate their trainees' process movement.*

Indexing Content Processing Skills

You should also be pleased if you have accomplished our *CPS* training skill objective: you are now capable of making a training content delivery in your specialty area. You can make a training delivery in any area where you have conquered the content.

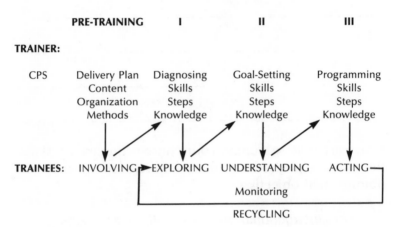

PHASES OF TRAINING

	PRE-TRAINING	I	II	III
TRAINER:				
CPS	Delivery Plan Content Organization Methods	Diagnosing Skills Steps Knowledge	Goal-Setting Skills Steps Knowledge	Programming Skills Steps Knowledge
TRAINEES:	INVOLVING	EXPLORING	UNDERSTANDING	ACTING

Monitoring

RECYCLING

Summarizing Content Processing Skills

Our expertise in our *CPS* is what enables us to develop training and learning programs. Because our content is developed and organized around skilis, we are able to program every trainee's experience. Each trainee becomes a unique entity, with his or her own unique starting point for training. Effective trainers train trainees, and we are effective trainers. We deliver content to trainees. Our training delivery is totally dependent upon moment-to-moment diagnosis of the trainees' performances. We do not take still and static photos of living, learning, and working processes. We take continuous and ongoing motion pictures of the trainee in interaction with the content. These motion pictures enable every trainee to succeed in every training effort. Our trainees cannot fail, because they begin where they are, and move to where they can go. They cannot fail because they are learning. Our *CPS* are based upon the moment-to-moment relationship of the trainees with the content. They are also based upon the moment-to-moment relationship of the trainer with the trainees. The interpersonal relationship between the trainer and trainees is the topic of the next chapter.

References

Berenson, D. H., Berenson, S. R. and Carkhuff, R. R. *The Skills of Teaching—Teaching Delivery Skills.* Amherst, Mass.: Human Resource Development Press, 1979.

Campbell, J. P. "Personnel Training and Development." *Annual Review of Psychology,* 1977, *22,* 565-602.

Carkhuff, R. R. and Berenson, D. H. *The Skilled Teacher.* Amherst, Mass.: Human Resource Development Press, 1981.

Clark, D.C. "Teaching Concepts in the Classroom." *Journal of Educational Psychology,* 1971, *62,* 253-278.

Cornwell, J. B. "Test Before You Train." *Training,* 1981, *18,* 40-42.

Flanders, N.A. "Diagnosing and Utilizing Social Structures in Classroom Learning." In *Dynamics of Instructional Groups.* National Society for the Study of Education, 59th Yearbook, Part II. Chicago, Ill.: University of Chicago Press, 1960.

Flanders, N. A. "Teacher Influence in the Classroom: Research on Classroom Climate." In *Theory and Research in Teaching.* Edited by A. Bellack. New York: Columbia Teacher's College, 1963.

Gagne, R. M. *Conditions of Learning.* New York: Holt, Rinehart and Winston, 1977.

Gilbert, T. F. *Human Competence.* New York: McGraw-Hill, 1978.

Hills, S. M. *How Craftsmen Learn Their Skills.* Washington, D.C.: National Institute of Education, 1981.

Hudgins, B. B. *Self-Contained Training Materials for Teacher Education.* Bloomington, Ind.: National Center for the Development of Training Materials in Teacher Education, Indiana University, 1974.

Kaya, E., Gerhard, M., Staslewski, A. and Berenson, D. H. *Developing a Theory of Educational Practices for the Elementary School.* Norwalk, Conn.: Ford Foundation Fund for the Improvement of Education, 1967.

Mager, R. F. and Beach, K.M. *Developing Vocational Objectives.* San Francisco, Calif.: Fearon-Pitman, 1966.

Miller, W. R. and Rose, H. C. *Instructors and Their Jobs.* Chicago, Ill.: American Technical Society, 1977.

Nadler, L. *Designing Training Programs.* Reading, Mass.: Addison-Wesley, 1982.

O'Neil, H. F. and Speilburger, C. *Cognitive and Affective Learning Strategies.* New York: Academic Press, 1978.

Pfeiffer, I. L. "Teaching in Ability-Grouped English Classes: A Study of Verbal Interaction and Cognitive Goals." *Journal of Teacher Education*, 1966, *17*, No. 3.

Ribler, R.I. *Training and Development Guide.* Reston, Va.: Reston Publishing Co., 1983.

4

Interpersonal Processing Skills

Perhaps the most important set of skills that any one human being can have is the ability to relate to another human being. The most effective way of relating is to process interpersonally with that other human: to facilitate the exploring, understanding, and acting of the other person. The active ingredients that serve to facilitate or retard human relationships and human development are interpersonal. Depending upon the level of concession by the trainees, the trainers may have dramatically constructive or destructive effects upon the trainees. Interpersonal skills enable a person to "walk in another's moccasins": to see the world through the other's eyes and communicate what is seen; to assist the other person in processing to surmount the problems and achieve the goals. Interpersonal processing skills emphasize the internal frames of reference of the trainees as they move through the training experience. These skills enable the trainer to relate the trainees' frames of reference to the training goals. They are the catalysts that activate the trainees to receive all other training ingredients.

A number of studies have shown that teachers' and trainers' interpersonal skills relate to the learners' and trainees' academic and vocational as well as social achievement. In particular, effective interpersonal skills can be summarized as attending or paying attention (Cantril, 1957; Carkhuff, 1983; Carkhuff and Berenson, 1981; Carkhuff, Berenson and Pierce, 1977; Steiner, 1972); responding or being empathic with the trainees' frames of reference (Argyris, 1967; Aspy, 1972; Aspy and Roebuck, 1977; Bloom, Englehart, Furst, Hill, and Krathwohl, 1956; Carkhuff, 1969, 1971; Flanders, 1970; Ryan, 1960); personalizing or being additive in understanding the trainees' problems or goals (Carkhuff, 1983; Carkhuff and Berenson, 1981; Solomon, Rosenberg and Berdele, 1964); individualizing or initiating programs to meet the trainees' unique needs (Carkhuff, 1983; Carkhuff and Berenson, 1981; Rosenshine, 1971); and reinforcing the trainees from their own internal frames of reference (Aspy and Roebuck, 1977; Gage, 1977; Knowles, 1977; Neff, 1968). The basic principle of interpersonal skills is that all productive learning or training begins with the trainees' frames of reference.

Principles of Interpersonal Processing Skills

Our interpersonal processing skills *(IPS)* training objective in this lesson is as follows:

The instructional trainees will make training deliveries by implementing interpersonal processing skills under formal and informal conditions and at levels that facilitate their trainees' process movement.

Before you learn interpersonal processing skills, you may want an index of your skills in this area. Perhaps you can take a training skill objective in your specialty content and outline the interpersonal processes you would use to facilitate the achievement of this objective.

_____

_____

_____

_____

_____

Indexing Interpersonal Processing Skills

You should be pleased if you emphasized relating to the trainees' frames of reference. These *IPS* will include attending to the trainees, responding to the trainees' frames of reference, personalizing the trainees' goals, individualizing the trainees' programs, and reinforcing the training process.

ATTENDING: To the trainees in order to involve them in training.

RESPONDING: To the trainees in order to facilitate their exploring.

PERSONALIZING: The trainees' experiences in order to facilitate their understanding.

INDIVIDUALIZING: Programs in order to facilitate trainee acting.

REINFORCING: The training in order to facilitate trainee recycling.

PHASES OF TRAINING

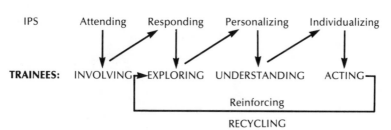

Overviewing Interpersonal Processing Skills

Attending to the Trainees

We prepare for our training delivery by attending to our trainees. Attending means being attentive or paying attention to our trainees, or simply caring about what happens to them. When attending, we poise ourselves in order to cover the trainees with a "hovering attentiveness," just as we do with an infant. When we provide our trainees with our full and undivided attention, we are initiating the principle of reciprocal effect: the trainees give us, in return, their full and undivided attention. The trainees give us the input which we need to initiate the training delivery process. Attending involves the trainees in the training process. By attending to the trainees we communicate an interest in their welfare. We also receive input and feedback concerning the effectiveness of the training experience from the things we see and hear our trainees do and say.

Attending

Attending physically means that we posture ourselves in such a way as to give our trainees our full and undivided attention. It means that we are "with them." It is precisely this type of attention that we expect from our trainees with regard to the training experience. For example, in relation to our trainee or group of trainees, we position ourselves at the vertex of a right angle incorporating both extreme perimeters of the trainees in our presence. This method of positioning is often referred to as "squaring." Similarly, we lean forward or toward our trainees, just as we do with all things in which we are interested. Finally, we make frequent eye contact with all of our trainees. Practice these attending skills in groups of two or three. What other ways can you attend to your trainees? We attend to our trainees in their absence when we develop and organize our content. We attend to our trainees in their presence when we posture ourselves to attend physically to them, observe them, and listen to them. All of these attending skills serve to involve the trainee in the training process.

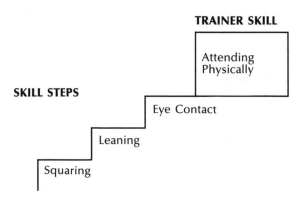

Attending Physically to the Trainees

Observing means being able to "see" the appearance and behavior of trainees, which give you clues to their experience: instead of a crowd of faces, you see a frown, a grin, a pair of eyes that follow you in eager anticipation of learning something. One way of observing both appearance and behavior is for us to watch the trainees' physical attending skills. That is, we observe the trainees' squaring, leaning, and eyeing behavior. We can make inferences from these cues. Physically, we can infer whether the trainees have high, moderate, or low levels of energy. Emotionally and interpersonally, we can infer whether they are "up," neutral, or "down." Intellectually, we can infer whether they have a high, moderate, or low level of readiness for training. Practice using these observing skills in a small group. What other dimensions can you observe in your trainees?

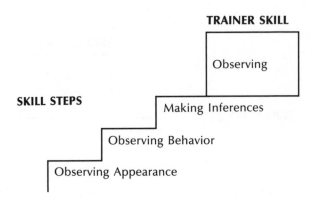

Observing the Trainees

Listening means being able to "hear" what has been said, and how it has been said, in order to understand the trainees' experiences. Instead of a babble of voices, we pick out this trainee's calm and assured comment, or another's hesitant and embarrassed question. The skill steps involved in listening include at least the following: suspending our own judgments, i.e., not listening to ourselves; resisting all distractions in order to focus upon the expression of the trainees; and recalling the content of the trainees' verbal expressions. These skill steps will insure that we have at least heard the content of the trainees' expressions. Practice repeating verbatim the content of the trainees' expressions. What other dimensions are involved in listening?

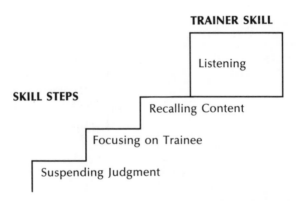

Listening to the Trainees

In summary, attending involves at least three skills: attending physically in order to pay attention to the trainees, observing in order to "see" the trainees, and listening in order to "hear" the trainees. In addition, attending physically prepares us for observing, and observing prepares us for listening. These attending skills, when employed simultaneously, will involve the trainees in the training process. At this point, you will want to practice using these skills simultaneously. First, practice attending physically, observing, and listening with people, like yourselves, who are committed to learning training skills. Then apply these skills in your training sessions with your trainees. You are sure to experience the principle of reciprocal effect: the trainees will attend constructively to you to the same degree that you attend constructively to them.

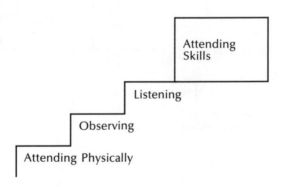

Practicing Attending

Responding to the Trainees

Responding is the key interpersonal ingredient. Responding means communicating an understanding of the experiences expressed by the trainees. Responding means that we empathically enter the experiences of the trainees—sit in their seats, see the experiences through their eyes—and communicate to them our understanding of those experiences. When we respond to the trainees' experiences we are accomplishing two essential training purposes: 1) we are coming into contact with the trainees' frames of reference; and 2) we are bringing the trainees into contact with their own frames of reference. Again, the most fundamental principle of training is that all learning or training begins with the trainees' frames of reference.

Our responsiveness is the way we enter the trainees' experiences and communicate to them our understanding of their points of view. Responding initiates the first phase of training. After involving the trainees in the training process through attending, we now facilitate their exploration through responding. Responding skills are employed simultaneously with the diagnostic delivery skills to facilitate the trainees' exploration. The responding skills allow us to enter the trainees' internal frames of reference. The diagnostic skills serve to assess the trainees from an external frame of reference—the trainer's. Both the responding and the diagnostic skills converge to facilitate the trainees' exploration of where they are in the training experience. The point at which the trainees begin their training program is now clear to both trainer and trainees, from both an internal and external frame of reference.

Responding

The first way of responding to our trainees is to communicate our understanding of the content they are expressing. We can capture the content of an expression by repeating it verbatim. With more lengthy expressions, we can repeat the gist or the common theme. For example, a group of trainees might say the following:

"New task assignments are always like that. They don't really tell you what to do."

When responding to content, we can recall the content by repeating the expression verbatim to ourselves. Then we can communicate our grasp of the content by reflecting the gist of it to the trainees, using the reflective format, "You're saying _____." For example, we might respond to the content in the above expression as follows:

"You're saying that the instructions don't tell what to do."

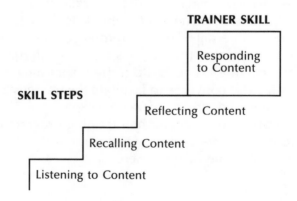

Responding to Content

The second way of responding to our trainees is to communicate our understanding of the trainees' feelings about their experiences. Both trainers and trainees are often reluctant to enter the realm of feelings. This is largely because trainers have not been taught to do so, and when they try they are often inaccurate and thus ineffective. They tend to introduce their own feelings prematurely and out of context. Thus, trainers say things like "you shouldn't feel that way," or "that's not the way it is," long before they have given the trainees a chance to explore their experiences. We can capture the feelings of an experience by doing three simple things: 1) repeating the expression verbatim to ourselves just as the trainees expressed themselves to us; 2) asking ourselves, as if we were trainees, "How would that make me feel?"; and 3) using the reflective format for communicating the feeling, i.e., "You feel _____."

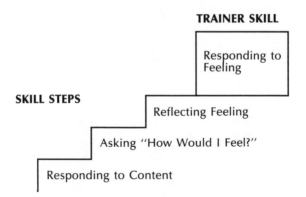

Responding to Feeling

For example, when the trainees state that the instructions do not tell them what to do, the trainer might respond as follows: "You feel frustrated." On the following page is the beginning of a list of basic categories of feeling words at strong, mild, and weak levels of intensity. Work with other individuals interested in learning training skills in order to practice responding to feeling, and to expand your repertoire of feeling words. When you feel confident in your responding skills, then try to apply them in your training sessions.

Expanding Feeling Words

CATEGORIES OF FEELINGS

LEVELS OF INTENSITY	Confused	Strong	Weak	Happy	Sad	Angry	Scared
Strong	Bewildered Trapped Troubled	Potent Super Powerful	Overwhelmed Impotent Small	Excited Elated Overjoyed	Hopeless Sorrowful Depressed	Furious Seething Enraged	Fearful Panicky Afraid
Mild	Disorganized Mixed-Up Foggy	Energetic Confident Capable	Incapable Helpless Insecure	Cheerful Up Good	Upset Distressed Down	Annoyed Frustrated Agitated	Threatened Insecure Uneasy
Weak	Bothered Uncomfortable Undecided	Sure Secure Durable	Shaky Unsure Soft	Glad Content Satisfied	Sorry Lost Bad	Uptight Dismayed Put Out	Timid Unsure Nervous

"Somehow," you may say, "the response to feeling seems incomplete."

"You're feeling confused because the response seems incomplete," is the response to make to such an expression.

Exactly! The response to the trainee's experience is incomplete without the meaning or the reason for the feeling. The response to feeling must be complemented by the reason for the feeling. To develop our response to meaning we need only to: 1) build upon our feeling response; and 2) draw upon the content of the expression, asking ourselves the reason for the feeling. It remains only to use the reflective format to respond to the feeling and meaning, "You feel _____ because _____." For example, we might formulate the following response to the trainees who stated that instructions didn't tell them what to do: "You feel frustrated because the instructions don't give you what you need to know." This is a complete response to the trainees' experience. It captures the feeling and the meaning.

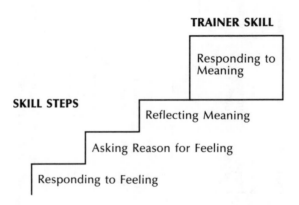

TRAINER SKILL

Responding to Meaning

SKILL STEPS

Reflecting Meaning

Asking Reason for Feeling

Responding to Feeling

Responding to Meaning

In summary, our responding skills involve at least three skill areas: responding to the content of the trainees' expressions, responding to the feeling of the trainees' experiences, and responding to the meaning of the trainees' experiences. Each response prepares us for the next response. The responses to feeling and meaning culminate in a complete response to the trainees' experiences. Responding accurately means that we are interchangeable in our understanding of the trainees' frames of reference. By responding accurately, we have facilitated the trainees' exploration of where they are in relation to their training experiences. At this point, you will want to practice using all of your responsive skills simultaneously. Practice using these skills in a simulated training setting, then apply the responding skills in your actual training sessions.

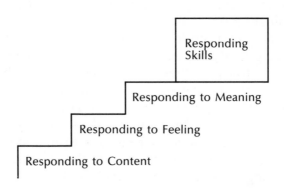

Practicing Responding

Personalizing the Training Experience

Personalizing provides the transition from exploration to individualized action or training programs. Personalizing means individualizing the goals of training. Personalizing means that we enter the trainees' perceptions in order to develop goals that come from their frames of reference. When we personalize the trainees' understanding of their experiences, we accomplish two essential training purposes: 1) we relate the trainees' frames of reference to training goals, and 2) we establish individualized goals that will guide the development of our individualized training programs. Our personalizing skills will enable us to extend the trainees' frames of reference into goals that have value for the trainees. Our personalizing skills will allow us to develop training programs that will enable our trainees to achieve their training goals.

Personalizing introduces the second phase of training. After responding to the trainees' experiences in order to facilitate their exploration of where they are, we now personalize their understanding of their experiences. Personalizing helps the trainees understand where they are in relation to where they want or need to be in their training experiences. Personalizing skills are used simultaneously with our goal-setting skills to facilitate the trainees' understanding. The personalizing skills serve to extend the trainees' internal frames of reference to an understanding of the externally derived goals. Both the personalizing and goal-setting skills converge to facilitate the trainees' understanding of where they want or need to be in the training experience. The goal of the training program is therefore clear to trainer and trainees from both an external, diagnostic frame of reference and also the trainees' internal frames of reference.

Personalizing

When we responded to the experiences of the trainees, we did so at the level the trainees themselves expressed. We attempted to respond interchangeably with the feeling and meaning of their experiences. In so doing, we allowed the trainees to externalize the meanings or the reasons for the feelings. We accepted the trainees in the manner they presented themselves. Now we are going to go beyond the trainees' presentations. We do this by personalizing the meaning for the trainees by stating the implications of the situation. In so doing, we internalize the trainees' responsibility for their experiences. For example, we responded to the meaning of the trainees' experiences when we said, "You feel frustrated because the instructions don't tell you what you need to know." Now we ask a question concerning the personal implications for the trainees: "What are the implications of the experience for them?" Foremost among the implications is the fact that the trainees did not do well on the newly assigned tasks. We communicate this internalized meaning with the format: "You feel _____ because you _____." Thus we may personalize our response to meaning as follows: "You feel frustrated because you didn't do well on your new assignments." Practice making personalized responses to meaning in simulated training groups, rotating the roles of supervisor, trainer, and trainees.

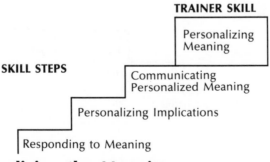

SKILL STEPS

TRAINER SKILL

Personalizing Meaning

Communicating Personalized Meaning

Personalizing Implications

Responding to Meaning

Personalizing the Meaning

Having personalized and internalized the meaning of the trainees' experiences, we now want to personalize the problem. After all, the trainees' problems are obstacles to be removed by training. We can personalize the problem by identifying the trainees' deficits. To do this, we ask ourselves the following question, as if we were the trainees: "What is it that I lack that led to this situation?" For example, we personalized the meaning of the trainees' experiences with our response, "You feel frustrated because you didn't do well on your new assignments." Now, we answer the deficit question for the trainees: the trainees lack the ability to handle new tasks effectively. It remains for us to communicate this response deficit with the format, "You feel _____ because you cannot _____." Thus, to continue the example, we may personalize the problem as follows: "You feel frustrated because you can't handle these new tasks." The response personalizes the problem for the trainees. Practice making personalized responses to problems in simulated training groups, rotating the roles of supervisor, trainer, and trainees.

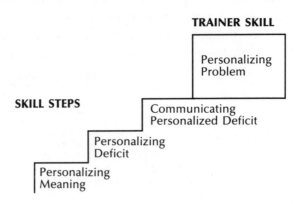

Personalizing the Problem

After personalizing the problem, we must personalize the feeling. Our trainees now have a different perception of the problem than they began with. The meaning has changed. For one thing, the trainees have become accountable for their contribution to the situation. And so the feeling may change. We personalize the feeling the same way that we responded to feeling. We ask the question, "How does that make me feel?" just as if we were the trainees. For example, we personalized the trainee's problem when we said: "You feel frustrated because you cannot handle these tasks." Now, we answer the new training question for the trainees: Do the trainees feel frustrated? Or do the trainees feel disappointed? Most personalized feeling responses conclude in disappointment in oneself. It remains for us to communicate this personalized feeling with the same format as the personalized problem: "You feel _____ because you cannot _____." Thus, to continue the example, we can personalize the feeling as follows: "You feel disappointed in yourself because you cannot handle these new tasks." The response personalizes the new feeling for the trainees. Practice making personalized feeling responses in simulated training groups, rotating the roles of supervisor, trainer, and trainees.

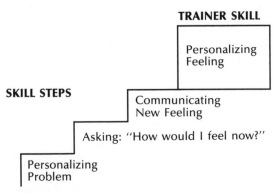

Personalizing the Feeling

Finally, we must personalize the goal. The problem, after all, dictates the goal. Indeed, the goal is simply the flip-side of the problem. The way we personalize the goal is to make explicit the goal that is implied by the personalized problem. For example, we personalized the trainee's problem and feeling when we said: "You feel disappointed in yourself because you cannot handle these new tasks." Now we simply append an explicit statement of the goal. We do this by adding the goal statement: "...and you really want to." Thus, to continue our example, we may personalize the goal as follows: "You feel disappointed in yourself because you cannot handle these new tasks and you really want to." Such a response is a personalized goal statement. Practice making personalized goal responses in simulated training groups, rotating the roles of supervisor, trainer, and trainees.

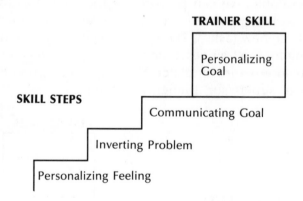

Personalizing the Goal

In summary, our personalizing skills involve at least four skill areas: personalizing meaning; personalizing problems; personalizing feelings; and personalizing goals. Each personalized response prepares us for the next response, just as responding to feeling and meaning prepared us for personalizing. By personalizing the trainees' goals, we have gone beyond the trainees' expressions. We have facilitated the trainees' understanding of where they are in relation to where they want to be in the training experience. At this point, you will want to practice using our personalizing skills. Only now, unlike responding, you will use these skills sequentially. You will lay a base using responsive skills that are interchangeable with your trainees' expressions. Then, you will move sequentially through your personalizing skills. You should always be careful to check your accuracy with your interchangeable responses to feeling and meaning. After you have practiced these skills in simulated training groups, then you can apply them in your actual training sessions.

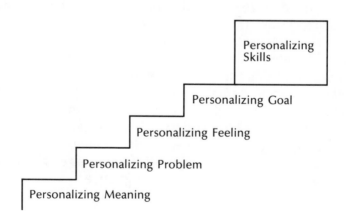

Practicing Personalizing

Individualizing the Trainees' Programs

The training process culminates in an individualized action or training program. Individualizing means tailoring the training programs to meet the trainees' unique needs. Individualizing means entering each trainee's perception in order to relate that individualized frame of reference to a training program. When we individualize the trainee's action programs, we accomplish two essential training purposes: 1) we relate the trainees' frames of reference to the training programs, and 2) we relate the trainees' frames of reference to individualized reinforcements for achievement of the training programs. Our individualizing skills will enable us to help the trainees to conclude the training process. They will allow us to develop truly individualized training programs that will enable our trainees to achieve their training goals.

Individualizing introduces the third phase of training. Having personalized the trainees' goals in order to facilitate their understanding of where they want or need to be, we now individualize their action programs to get there. Individualizing skills are used simultaneously with our programming skills to facilitate the trainees' actons. The individualizing skills serve to extend the trainees' internal frames of reference so that they can relate to the externally derived action programs. Both the individualizing and programming skills converge to facilitate the trainees' acting to get from where they are to where they want or need to be. The steps of the training program are clear to trainer and trainees from both our external, diagnostic frames of reference and the trainees' internal frames of reference.

Individualizing

When we personalized the goal for the trainees, we captured their disappointment in their response deficits and transformed their problems into goal statements. It remains for us to individualize their training goals. We individualize the training goals by translating them into training principles. Each trainee can do this by developing an individualized training principle that incorporates the skill to be learned, the particular application to be made, and the unique human benefit to be achieved. To do this, we use the following format for individualized training principles: "If (skill), then (application) so that (benefit)." For example, we personalized the training goal for our trainees: "You feel disappointed in yourself because you cannot handle these new tasks and you really want to." Now we will individualize the training goal with an individualized training principle: "If you learn to use instructions (skill), then you will be able to perform these new tasks (application) so that you can learn to contribute to unit productivity." Such a response is an individualized training goal statement. By achieving the skill, the trainee can make the unique application and receive the unique benefit. Practice making individualized training goal statements in simulated training groups, rotating the roles of supervisors, trainers, and trainees.

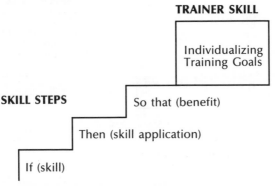

TRAINER SKILL

Individualizing Training Goals

SKILL STEPS

So that (benefit)

Then (skill application)

If (skill)

Individualizing Training Goals

Having an individualized training goal statement allows us to individualize the sequencing of the training. Most programs are comprised of steps that are sequenced consecutively or by contingency where each step is dependent upon the performance of the previous step. Some trainees cannot perform the steps as they are designed. They require programs individualized to their own particular training or processing styles. The modes of individualizing include sequencing the steps from simple-to-complex, concrete-to-abstract, and immediate-to-remote. Often these steps vary with those sequenced by contingency as well as with each other. For example, an interpersonal skills program could begin with each trainee facing another individual, a most simple step that can be performed readily. Or the same interpersonal skills program could begin with developing programs, the most concrete steps. Or the same interpersonal skills program could begin by responding to real-life problems, the most immediate experience. Practice individualizing training sequencing in simulated training groups. Try to develop additional methods of sequencing: these different methods allow us to further individualize the training programs.

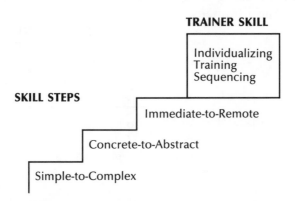

Individualizing Training Sequencing

We can further individualize the training programs by individualizing the training steps. The training steps emphasize what the trainee has to do, know, and feel. Perhaps the trainee can perform two of these steps but not the third. The trainee may be able to do the step but does not understand the supportive knowledge involved. Or the trainee may be able to do and understand a step but has a negative attitude toward performing it. Task performance skills, for example, may involve preparing, performing, and producing (doing); technical expertise (knowing); and motivation and confidence (feeling). Thus, to fully individualize training steps we need to emphasize the trainee's internalized training steps in much the same manner that we developed the external steps.

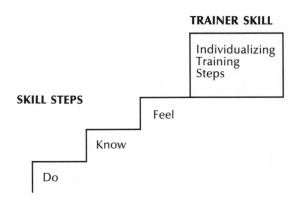

Individualizing Training Steps

In summary, our task of individualizing training programs involves at least three skills: individualizing training goals, individualizing training sequencing, and individualizing training steps. Each individualized training program prepares us for the next individualized training program. By individualizing the training programs, we have facilitated the trainees' acting to get from where they are to where they want or need to be. At this point, you may need to practice using your individualizing skills. Be careful to relate the internal frames of reference of the trainees to the external frame of reference of the content. After you have practiced these individualizing skills in simulated training groups, then apply them in your actual training sessions.

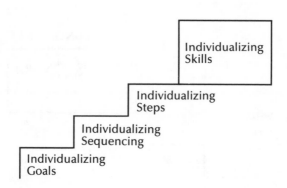

Practicing Individualizing

Reinforcing the Trainees

We have developed an individualized training program. We did this by putting together programs drawn from both the trainees' internalized frames of reference and the externalized frame of reference present in the content. It only remains to reinforce the achievement of each step in the training program. The reinforcement of training flows directly from the trainees' frames of reference as did the individualized training program. Indeed, the most potent reinforcement will be the long-term benefits that will accrue to the trainees by learning the skills. The potency of the trainer's reinforcement is related directly to the empathy the trainer has for the trainees. Reinforcing serves to introduce the post-training phase or recycling of training. Having individualized the training programs to get the trainees from where they are to where they want to be, we now individualize the reinforcements to get them there. Reinforcing skills are used simultaneously with our monitoring skills to stimulate the recycling of training. The reinforcing skills serve to strengthen the skills applications that are monitored. The reinforcing skills also enhance the skill steps and supportive knowledge needed to acquire and apply the skill. Together, the reinforcing and monitoring skills insure the correct application of the skill, requisite to the next cycle of training.

Reinforcing

The trainer uses his or her interpersonal skills to reinforce training. The trainer simply makes a personalized response to the trainees' experiences based upon monitoring the skill application. In so doing, the trainer's task is to show the trainees how learning each new skill, and making each new application, leads to the long-term benefit. Thus, the trainer personalizes the response by using the individualized training principle:

> "You feel _____ because you can (skill application) so that you (benefit)."

Thus, for example, we might use the following positively reinforcing phrase with the trainees in our illustration:

> "You feel good because you are performing the new tasks so that you can now move toward your productivity goals."

Such a response captures the feeling accompanying an effective skill application. It also complements the meaning of the skill application with the long-term benefit for the trainees. This positively reinforcing response can also be used for the training of skill steps and supportive knowledge, during either the cycling or recycling of training. Practice making positively reinforcing responses in simulated training groups, rotating the roles of supervisor, trainer, and trainees.

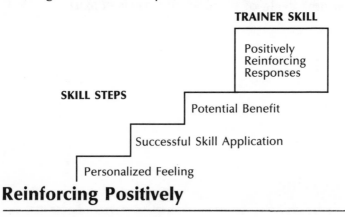

TRAINER SKILL

Positively Reinforcing Responses

SKILL STEPS

Potential Benefit

Successful Skill Application

Personalized Feeling

Reinforcing Positively

Obviously not all skill applications are satisfactorily discharged by all trainees. Clearly, the trainer must use interpersonal skills to make a personalized response to the problems the trainees are encountering. As with positive reinforcements, the trainer will use the skill application and benefit to make negatively reinforcing responses:

"You feel _____ because you cannot (skill application) so that you are not (benefit)."

Thus, for example, we might use the following negatively reinforcing phrase with the trainees in our illustration:

"You feel bad because you cannot perform the tasks so that you are not moving toward your productivity goal."

Such a response captures the feeling and the problem of the trainees' experiences. It does not punish the trainees for their efforts, however feeble. It puts the training effort in the trainees' hands by personalizing the response from the trainees' frames of reference. This negatively reinforcing response can also be used for negatively reinforcing training skill steps and supportive knowledge. Practice making negatively reinforcing responses in simulated training groups, rotating the roles of supervisor, trainer, and trainees.

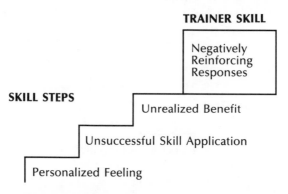

TRAINER SKILL

Negatively Reinforcing Responses

SKILL STEPS

Unrealized Benefit

Unsuccessful Skill Application

Personalized Feeling

Reinforcing Negatively

Finally, it is sometimes unclear to the trainer whether or not the trainees are making effective skill applications. This is usually because the trainees, themselves, are not clear. It may require intense vigilance and fine discrimination on the trainer's part to make the determination. Ultimately, it must be determined before the trainees move on to new training: either the trainees have made the skill application or not. Accordingly, the trainer will either make a positively or negatively reinforcing response. In any event, the trainer can use the interpersonal skills to respond to the trainees' experience at the moment:

"You feel _____ because sometimes you can and sometimes you cannot (skill application) so that you are not clear about (benefit)."

Thus, we might respond to the trainees' mixed experience:

"You feel confused because you are performing some tasks and not others, so that you are not clear about your movement toward your productivity goals."

Such a response comes from the trainee's frames of reference, yet allows the trainer time to observe the trainee's performances. It can also be used for the training of skill steps and supportive knowledge. Practice vigilant responses in simulated training groups, using different role play situations.

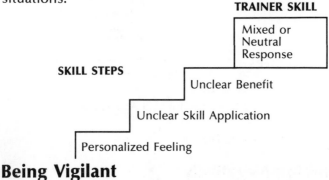

Being Vigilant

In summary, our individualized reinforcing skills involve at least three skills: making positively reinforcing responses, making negatively reinforcing responses, and making mixed or neutral responses. Each reinforcing response comes from the trainees' own unique frames of reference. It incorporates the trainees' feelings, skill applications, and benefits.

At this point, practice using your reinforcing skills. Always emphasize observing the trainees' performances vigilantly, in order to determine whether it is moving them toward or away from the skill application and the human benefit. After you have practiced these reinforcing skills in simulated training groups, then you will want to apply them in your actual training sessions.

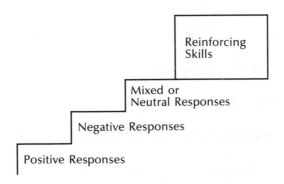

Practicing Reinforcing

Exercising

Again, we employ our interpersonal processing skills, *IPS*, to facilitate the trainees' movements through E-U-A. We can use *IPS* for facilitating training when "thinking on our feet," in or out of our training sessions. We can apply the *IPS* in any critical situation that involves human relations in general, i.e., at home and school, as well as work. We can also train our trainees in the basic *IPS* so that they can relate to others in facilitating their own and others' learning experiences.

SKILL OBJECTIVE:

Trainees will communicate interpersonally under formal and informal conditions at levels of communication that facilitate the E-U-A of others by learning interpersonal processing skills.

ATTENDING:	Skills, steps, knowledge
RESPONDING:	Skills, steps, knowledge
PERSONALIZING:	Skills, steps, knowledge
INDIVIDUALIZING:	Skills, steps, knowledge
REINFORCING:	Skills, steps, knowledge

Overviewing Interpersonal Processing Skills

You may wish to do a repeat exercise using your interpersonal processing skills. Apply your interpersonal processing skills to living or working contexts. Develop your own individualized training program for the following skills: attending, responding, personalizing, individualizing, and reinforcing.

SKILL OBJECTIVE:

_____

_____

_____

SKILL PROGRAM

    ATTENDING: _____

_____

    RESPONDING: _____

_____

    PERSONALIZING: _____

_____

INDIVIDUALIZING: _____

_____

    REINFORCING: _____

_____

Repeating Interpersonal Processing Skills

Describe how you might apply your interpersonal processing skills within a living or home setting, a learning or training setting, and a working or job setting. Try to identify as many applications as possible.

LIVING: _____

_____

_____

_____

LEARNING: _____

_____

_____

_____

WORKING: _____

_____

_____

_____

Applying Interpersonal Processing Skills

Summarizing

Perhaps you can now outline how you would use interpersonal skills in training in your specialty skill content. Simply outline the interpersonal process you would use to facilitate the achievement of your trainees' skill objectives.

_____

_____

_____

_____

_____

If you are able to outline your interpersonal processing skills, then we are delighted because we have achieved our training skill objective:

> *The instructional trainees will make training deliveries by implementing interpersonal processing skills under formal and informal conditions and at levels that facilitate their trainees' process movements.*

Indexing Interpersonal Processing Skills

You should also be pleased if you have accomplished your *IPS* training skill objective: you are now capable of using your interpersonal skills in your specialty skills content. You can use your interpersonal processing skills in any area where you have conquered the content.

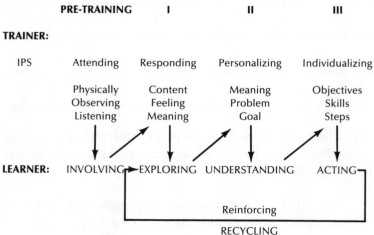

PHASES OF TRAINING

	PRE-TRAINING	I	II	III
TRAINER:				
IPS	Attending	Responding	Personalizing	Individualizing
	Physically	Content	Meaning	Objectives
	Observing	Feeling	Problem	Skills
	Listening	Meaning	Goal	Steps
LEARNER:	INVOLVING	EXPLORING	UNDERSTANDING	ACTING

Reinforcing

RECYCLING

Summarizing Interpersonal Processing Skills

In summary, interpersonal skills serve to engage the trainees in the training process: attending facilitates involvement, responding facilitates exploration, personalizing facilitates understanding, individualizing initiates action, and reinforcing recycles training. Interpersonal skills offer a comprehensive approach to relating trainers to the trainees' frames of reference. In conclusion, interpersonal skills enable us to assess the trainees' progress through their own eyes. In so doing, we can relate the trainees' internal frames of reference to the external frame of the skill content. Thus, we can be guided by what is effective in helping the trainees move through the phases of training. Our interpersonal skills enable us to converge objective reality with subjective experience.

References

Argyris, C. *The Nature of Competence-Acquisition Activities and Their Relation to Therapy.* New York: Association for Nervous and Mental Diseases, 1967.

Aspy, D. N. *Toward a Technology for Humanizing Education.* Champaign, Ill.: Research Press, 1972.

Aspy, D. N., and Roebuck, F. N. *KIDS Don't Learn From People They Don't Like.* Amherst, Mass.: Human Resource Development Press, 1977.

Bloom, B. S., Englehart, M. D., Furst, E. J., Hill, W. H., and Krathwohl, D. R. *A Taxonomy of Educational Objectives: Handbook I, The Cognitive Domain.* New York: Longmans, Green, 1956.

Cantril, H. "Perception and Interpersonal Relations." *American Journal Of Psychiatry*, 1957, *114*, 119-127.

Carkhuff, R. R. *Helping and Human Relations. Volumes I and II.* New York: Holt, Rinehart & Winston, 1969.

Carkhuff, R. R. *The Development of Human Resources.* New York: Holt, Rinehart & Winston, 1971.

Carkhuff, R. R. *The Art of Helping.* Amherst, Mass.: Human Resource Development Press, 1983.

Carkhuff, R. R., and Berenson, D. H. *The Skilled Teacher.* Amherst, Mass.: Human Resource Development Press, 1981.

Carkhuff, R. R., Berenson, D. H., and Pierce, R. M. *The Skills of Teaching—Interpersonal Skills.* Amherst, Mass.: Human Resource Development Press, 1977.

Flanders, N. A. *Analyzing Teaching Behavior.* Reading, Mass.: Addison-Wesley, 1970.

Gage, N. L. *The Scientific Basis of the Art of Teaching.* New York: Teachers College Press, 1977.

Knowles, M. "How Adults Learn." *Training*, 1977.

Neff, W. S. *Work as Human Behavior.* New York: Altheron Press, 1968.

Rosenshine, B. *Teaching Behaviors and Student Achievement.* London: National Foundation for Educational Research in England and Wales, 1971.

Ryan, D. G. *Characteristics of Teachers.* Washington, D.C.: American Council on Education, 1960.

Solomon, D., Rosenberg, L., and Berdele, W. E. "Teacher Behavior and Student Learning." *Journal of Educational Psychology*, 1969, *55*, 23-30.

Steiner, I. D. *Group Processes and Productivity.* New York: Academic Press, 1972.

5

Training Management Skills

Training management skills emphasize trainee processing within the implementation of the training delivery plan. Thus, where appropriate, trainees must explore, understand, and act upon their training experience within each of the stages of the content organization, i.e., Review, Overview, Presentation, Exercise, and Summary. The trainer employs content and interpersonal processing skills simultaneously to facilitate trainee processing. Clearly, the better the trainer's content skills and knowledge, the more productive the content processing. Similarly, the better the trainer's repertoire of interpersonal responses, the more productive the interpersonal processing.

Training management emphasizes trainee processing within the training delivery. As such, training management skills *(TMS)* emphasize three sets of skills. First, *TMS* emphasize the development of the training delivery plan which is organized around trainee exercises and applications (Berenson, Berenson and Carkhuff, 1978; Berliner, 1977; Carkhuff and Berenson, 1981; French, et al., 1957; Gage, 1976, 1977; Kearney, 1953; Lumsdaine, 1964; Mager, 1962; Smith and Moore, 1962). Second, *TMS* emphasize the content processing skills that process the trainees in terms of the requirements of the content (Berenson, Berenson and Carkhuff, 1979; Clark, 1971; Flanders, 1960, 1963; Hudgins, 1974; Kaya, Gerhard, Staslewski and Berenson, 1967; Pfeiffer, 1966). Finally, *TMS* emphasize the interpersonal processing skills that process the content from the trainees' frames of reference (Aspy, 1972; Aspy and Roebuck, 1977; Bloom, Englehart, Furst, Hill and Krathwohl, 1956; Carkhuff, 1969, 1971, 1983; Carkhuff, Berenson and Pierce, 1977; Flanders, 1970; Gage, 1977). Together, the content and interpersonal processing skills converge to facilitate trainee processing within the stages of the training delivery plan.

Principles of Training Management

Our training management skills *(TMS)* training objective in this lesson is as follows:

> *The instructional trainees will make training deliveries by implementing training management skills under formal and informal conditions at levels that facilitate their trainees' skill performances.*

Before you learn training management skills, you may want an index of your skills in this area. Perhaps you can take a training skill objective in your specialty content and outline how you would employ training management skills to achieve this objective.

Indexing Training Management Skills

You should be pleased if you emphasized processing within your training delivery plan. Thus, the trainers will use content processing skills *(CPS)* and interpersonal processing skills *(IPS)* to facilitate trainee performance within each of the stages of the training delivery plan.

CONTENT ORGANIZATION

TRAINING METHODS	Review CS	Overview SA	Present SS	Exercise SS	Summarize SP
Tell	L	T & L	T	L	L
Show	L	T & L	T	L	L
Do	L	T & L	L	L	L

Acting
Understanding
Exploring

TRAINING MANAGEMENT

CS = Contingency Skills SP = Skill Performance
SA = Skill Applications L = Learner
SS = Skill Steps T = Trainer

Overviewing Training Management Skills

Managing Training in the Review

Trainers employ their training management skills *(TMS)* during the Review by processing both content and trainees. Thus, trainers employ their *CPS* to process the requirements of the content. Also, they use their *IPS* to process the experiences of the trainees. Trainers employ both *CPS* and *IPS* simultaneously to facilitate trainee exploring, understanding, and acting.

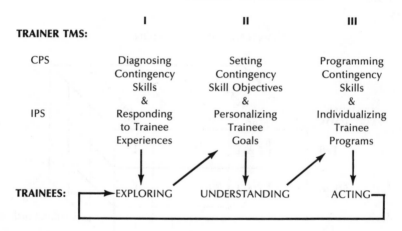

PHASES OF TRAINING

TRAINER TMS:	I	II	III
CPS	Diagnosing Contingency Skills	Setting Contingency Skill Objectives	Programming Contingency Skills
	&	&	&
IPS	Responding to Trainee Experiences	Personalizing Trainee Goals	Individualizing Trainee Programs
TRAINEES:	EXPLORING	UNDERSTANDING	ACTING

Thus, the trainer may diagnose the individual trainee's performance or nonperformance of the contingency skills *(CS)* in the Review. The nonperforming trainees are further diagnosed in terms of the skill step *(SS)* and/or supportive knowledge *(SK)* deficits. Objectives and programs may be developed and implemented accordingly until performance of the contingency skills is achieved. The trainees who can perform the contingency skills proceed to the Overview.

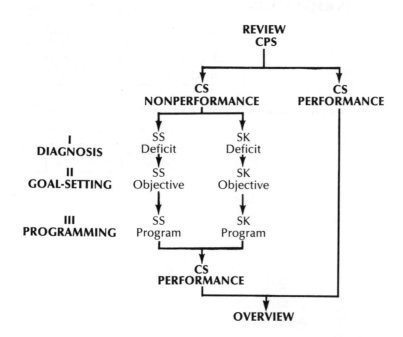

Content Processing in the Review

Simultaneously with the content processing, the trainer uses interpersonal skills to facilitate the processing of the trainees' experiences. In general, the trainer may use a variation of generic responding, personalizing, and individualizing formats:

RESPONDING: "You feel (good or bad) because you (did or did not) perform the skill."

PERSONALIZING: "You feel (pleased or disappointed) because you (can or cannot) perform the skill and you are eager to (move on to the next skill or learn this skill) ."

INDIVIDUALIZING: "If you learn to perform (skill) , then you will be able to make (skill application) so that you will achieve (human benefit) ."

Interpersonal Processing in the Review

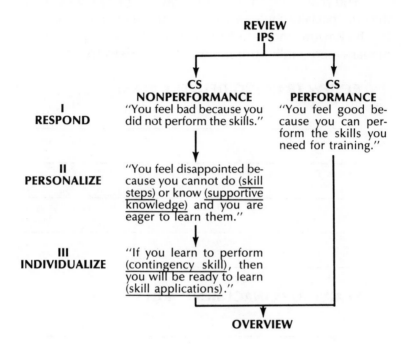

Interpersonal Processing in the Review

132

You may want to practice managing Review learning in your specialty content. Outline your training delivery plan for the Review. Indicate how you plan to use your training management skills to implement your delivery plan.

REVIEW TRAINING DELIVERY PLAN:

_____

_____

_____

_____

_____

TRAINING MANAGEMENT SKILLS:

_____

_____

_____

_____

_____

Practicing Training Management Skills in the Review

Managing Training in the Overview

Trainers continue to apply their training management skills during the Overview by processing both the content and the trainees' experiences. Thus, trainers employ their content and interpersonal processing skills simultaneously to facilitate trainee exploring, understanding, and acting. At the same time, the trainers *tell-show-do* potential skill applications in order to motivate the trainees to learn.

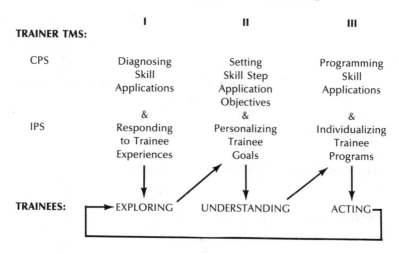

PHASES OF TRAINING

	I	II	III
TRAINER TMS:			
CPS	Diagnosing Skill Applications	Setting Skill Step Application Objectives	Programming Skill Applications
IPS	& Responding to Trainee Experiences	& Personalizing Trainee Goals	& Individualizing Trainee Programs
TRAINEES:	EXPLORING	UNDERSTANDING	ACTING

Managing Training in the Overview

The trainer may diagnose the individual trainee's ability to illustrate a skill application *(SA)* during the Overview. Non illustration elicits a further diagnosis focusing upon the deficits of contingency skills *(CS)* and/or images of skill application *(SA)*. In turn, objectives are set and programs developed and implemented until skill applications are illustrated. The trainees who can illustrate skill applications proceed to the Presentation.

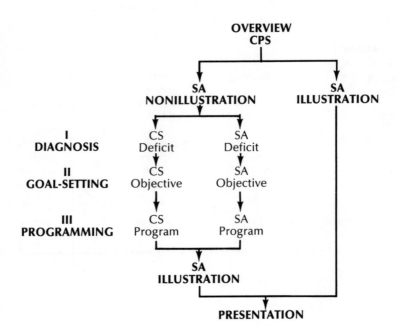

Content Processing in the Overview

Simultaneously, interpersonal processing is used to facilitate learning. The trainer responds to facilitate trainee exploration of the Overview experiences, personalizes to facilitate trainee understanding of the Overview goals, and individualizes to facilitate trainee acting upon the Overview programs.

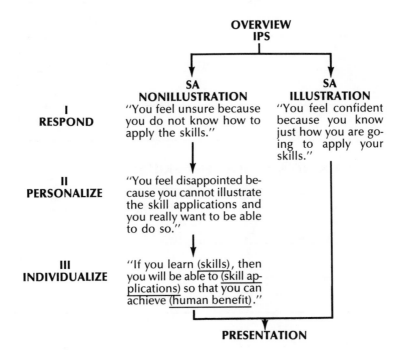

Interpersonal Processing in the Overview

You may want to practice managing Overview learning in your specialty content. Outline your training delivery plan for the Overview. Indicate how you plan to use your training management skills to implement your delivery plan.

OVERVIEW TRAINING DELIVERY PLAN:

_____

_____

_____

_____

_____

TRAINING MANAGEMENT SKILLS:

_____

_____

_____

_____

_____

Practicing Training Management Skills in the Overview

Managing Training in the Presentation

Trainers use their training management skills during the *doing* method of the Presentation. During the *tell* and *show* stages, the trainers emphasize their presentations while the trainees *hear* and *see* the reception. During the *do* stage, the trainers use their *CPS* and *IPS* to manage the trainees' performances of the skill steps to be learned.

PHASES OF TRAINING

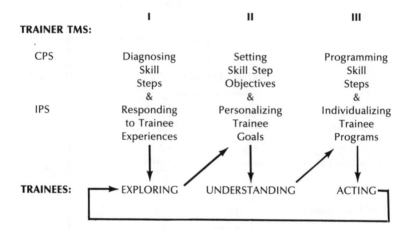

	I	II	III
TRAINER TMS:			
CPS	Diagnosing Skill Steps	Setting Skill Step Objectives	Programming Skill Steps
	&	&	&
IPS	Responding to Trainee Experiences	Personalizing Trainee Goals	Individualizing Trainee Programs
TRAINEES:	EXPLORING	UNDERSTANDING	ACTING

Managing Training in the Presentation

The trainer diagnoses skill step *(SS)* performance during the presentation. When the skill steps are not performed, the trainer further analyzes the skill step and/or supportive knowledge *(SK)* deficits. Objectives are set and training programs developed and implemented. The trainees who can perform the skill steps proceed to the Exercise stage.

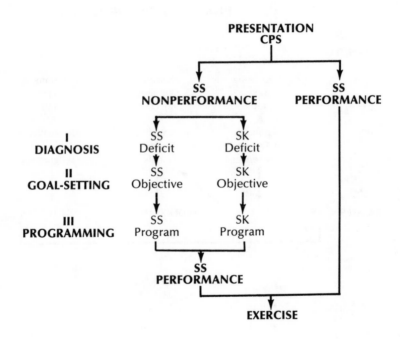

Content Processing in the Presentation

Simultaneously, the trainer uses interpersonal processing to facilitate learning in the Presentation by: responding to the trainees' experiences, personalizing training goals, and individualizing training programs.

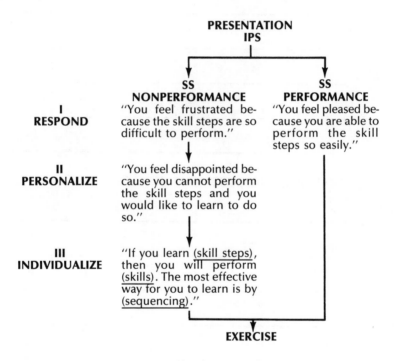

Interpersonal Processing in the Presentation

You may want to practice Presentation learning in your specialty content. Outline your Presentation training delivery plan and indicate how you plan to use your training management skills to implement it.

PRESENTATION TRAINING DELIVERY PLAN:

_____

_____

_____

_____

_____

TRAINING MANAGEMENT SKILLS:

_____

_____

_____

_____

_____

Practicing Training Management Skills in the Presentation

Managing Training in the Exercise

During the Exercise stage of training, the trainers manage trainee learning exclusively. The emphasis is upon trainee skill step performance. The trainers utilize all of their *CPS* and *IPS* to facilitate trainee processing or performance of the skill steps during the Exercise.

PHASES OF TRAINING

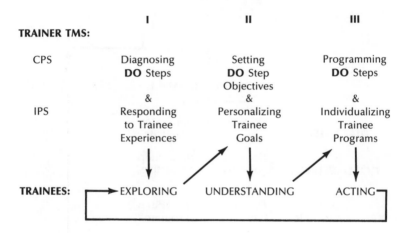

The trainer further diagnoses skill step *(SS)* performance during the Exercise stage. The exercises provide an opportunity to further analyze **do** and/or **think** step deficits, set training objectives, and develop training programs. The trainees who can perform the skill steps proceed to the Summary.

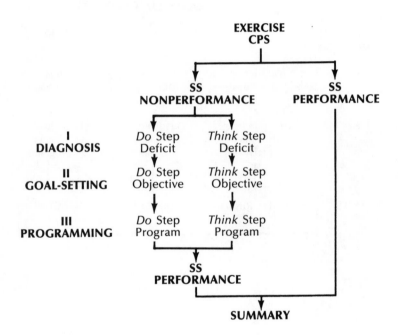

Content Processing in the Exercise

Simultaneously, the trainer will respond, personalize, and individualize to facilitate the trainee's processing of skill steps during the Exercise.

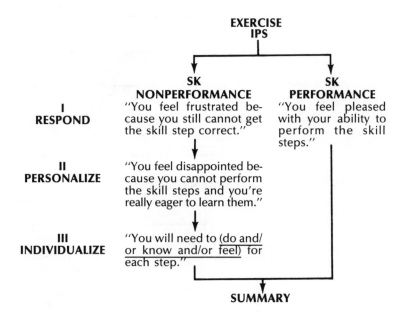

Interpersonal Processing in the Exercise

You may want to practice managing Exercise learning in your specialty content. Outline your training delivery plan for the Exercise. Indicate how you plan to use your training management skills to implement your delivery plan.

EXERCISE TRAINING DELIVERY PLAN:

_____

_____

_____

_____

_____

TRAINING MANAGEMENT SKILLS:

_____

_____

_____

_____

_____

Practicing Training Management Skills in the Exercise

Managing Training in the Summary

Trainers use their training delivery skills in the Summary to facilitate trainee processing of skill performance. Even during this post-training stage, the trainees may need to process their skill performance. Accordingly, the trainers use *CPS* and *IPS* simultaneously to facilitate trainee exploring, understanding, and acting.

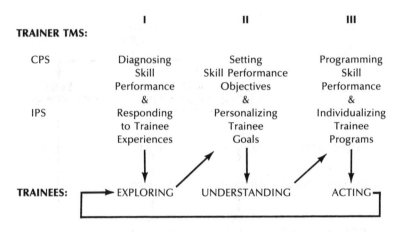

PHASES OF TRAINING

TRAINER TMS:	I	II	III
CPS	Diagnosing Skill Performance	Setting Skill Performance Objectives	Programming Skill Performance
	&	&	&
IPS	Responding to Trainee Experiences	Personalizing Trainee Goals	Individualizing Trainee Programs
TRAINEES:	EXPLORING	UNDERSTANDING	ACTING

Managing Training in the Summary

Finally, the trainer diagnoses skill performance during the Summary. Nonperformance requires further analysis of the skill step *(SS)* and/or supportive knowledge *(SK)* deficits, setting of skill step and/or supportive knowledge objectives, and development and implementation of skill step and/or supportive knowledge programs. Successful performance of the skills prepares the trainees for real-life applications and transfers.

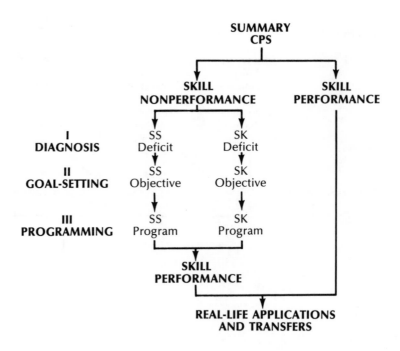

Content Processing in the Summary

Simultaneously, the trainer will respond, personalize, and individualize to facilitate the trainee's exploring, understanding, and acting upon skill performance during the Summary. If the trainee cannot perform to standards at the Summary, then the trainee must be recycled through the training process.

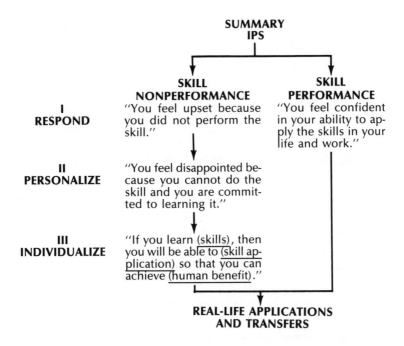

Interpersonal Processing in the Summary

You may want to practice managing *Summary* learning in your specialty skills content. Outline your training delivery plan for the *Summary*. Indicate how you will use your training management skills to implement your delivery plan.

SUMMARY TRAINING DELIVERY PLAN:

_____

_____

_____

_____

_____

TRAINING MANAGEMENT SKILLS:

_____

_____

_____

_____

_____

Practicing Training Management Skills in the Summary

Exercising

You now know how to use your training management skills to implement your training delivery plan. You can use your training management skills to train any material while "thinking on your feet," in or out of the training context. You can apply these skills in any critical situation that involves training and learning. For example, you can employ training management skills for teaching family members, employees, teachers, learners, or trainees to manage their own learning.

SKILL OBJECTIVE:

> Trainees will manage their own learning by using training management skills under real-life conditions at a level of effective applications.

TRAINING DELIVERY PLAN:	Content Development, Content Organization, Training Methods.
TRAINING MANAGEMENT SKILLS:	Content Processing, Interpersonal Processing.

Exercising Training Management Skills

You may wish to do a repeat exercise using your training management skills. Apply the training management skills to a variety of living, learning, or working contexts. Develop and implement your training delivery plan for these applications.

SKILL OBJECTIVE:

_____

_____

_____

TRAINING DELIVERY   _____
PLAN:

_____

_____

_____

TRAINING MANAGEMENT   _____
SKILLS:

_____

_____

_____

Repeating Training Management Skills

Describe how you might apply your training management skills within living, learning, and working settings. Try to identify as many applications as possible.

LIVING: _____

_____

_____

LEARNING: _____

_____

_____

WORKING: _____

_____

_____

Applying Training Management Skills

Summarizing
Perhaps you can now outline how you would employ your training management skills to implement your training delivery plan.

_____

_____

_____

_____

_____

You should feel confident if you are able to outline how you plan to implement your training delivery plan. A successful outline indicates that we have achieved our training skill objective.

> *The instructional trainees will make training deliveries by implementing training management skills under formal and informal conditions at levels that facilitate their trainees' skill performances.*

Indexing Training Management Skills

You should feel very pleased with your training management skills if you are able to manage the trainees' learning. Again, your training management skills emphasize using your *CPS* and *IPS simultaneously in conjunction with each other.*

TRAINING DELIVERY PLAN:
Content Development, Content Organization, Training Methods

TRAINING MANAGEMENT SKILLS:

CONTENT PROCESSING SKILLS: Diagnosing, Goal-Setting, Programming

INTERPERSONAL PROCESSING SKILLS: Responding, Personalizing, Individualizing

CONTENT ORGANIZATION

	Review	Overview	Present	Exercise	Summarize
TRAINING METHODS	CS	SA	SS	SS	SP
Tell	CPS	CPS	CPS	CPS	CPS
Show	&	&	&	&	&
	IPS	IPS	IPS	IPS	IPS
Do	L	T & L	T & L	L	L

Summarizing Training Management Skills

Managing the trainees' learning is the heart of the training delivery. It means that the trainer has responded to the trainees' frames of reference from both the external frame of reference of the content and the internal frames of reference of the trainees. Training management means that the trainer has "hooked up" the training content and the trainees in the ultimate outcome of training and development: the trainer has built the training experience around the recipients of the experience, the trainees who are going to go out and apply and transfer these skills to tasks in their real-life, world-of-work environment.

References

Aspy, D. N. *Toward a Technology for Humanizing Education.* Champaign, Ill. Research Press, 1972.

Aspy, D. N., and Roebuck, F. N. *KIDS Don't Learn From People They Don Like.* Amherst, Mass.: Human Resource Development Press, 1977.

Berenson, D. H., Berenson, S. R., and Carkhuff, R. R. *The Skills of Teaching—Lesson Planning Skills.* Amherst, Mass.: Human Resource Development Press, 1978.

Berenson, S. R., Berenson, D. H., and Carkhuff, R. R. *The Skills of Teaching—Teaching Delivery Skills.* Amherst, Mass.: Human Resource Development Press, 1979.

Berliner, D.C. *Instructional Time in Research on Teaching.* San Francisco: Far West Laboratory for Educational Research and Development, 1977.

Bloom, B. S., Englehart, M. D., Furst, E. J., Hill, W. H., and Krathwohl, D. R. *A Taxonomy of Educational Objectives: Handbook I, The Cognitive Domain.* New York: Longmans, Green, 1956.

Carkhuff, R. R. *Helping and Human Relations. Volumes I and II.* New York: Holt, Rinehart & Winston, 1969.

Carkhuff, R. R. *The Development of Human Resources.* New York: Holt, Rinehart & Winston, 1971.

Carkhuff, R. R. *The Art of Helping.* Amherst, Mass.: Human Resource Development Press, 1983.

Carkhuff, R. R., and Berenson, D.H. *The Skilled Teacher.* Amherst, Mass.: Human Resource Development Press, 1981.

Carkhuff, R. R., Berenson, D. H., and Pierce, R. M. *The Skills of Teaching—Interpersonal Skills.* Amherst, Mass.: Human Resource Development Press, 1977.

Clark, D. C. "Teaching Concepts in the Classroom." *Journal of Education Psychology,* 1971, *62,* 253-278.

Flanders, N. A. "Diagnosing and Utilizing Social Structures in Classroom Learning." In *The Dynamics of Instructional Groups,* National Society for the Study of Education, 59th Yearbook, Part II. Chicago: University of Chicago Press, 1960.

Flanders, N. A. "Teacher Influence in the Classroom: Research on Classroom Climate." In *Theory and Research in Teaching.* Edited by A. Bellack. New York: Columbia Teacher's College, 1963.

Flanders, N. A. *Analyzing Teaching Behavior.* Reading, Mass.: Addison-Wesley, 1970.

French, W., and Associates. *Behavioral Goals of General Education in High School.* New York: Russell Sage Foundation, 1957.

Gage, N. L., ed. *The Psychology of Teaching Methods.* Chicago: University of Chicago Press, 1976.

Gage, N. L. *The Scientific Basis of the Art of Teaching.* New York: Teachers College Press, 1977.

Hudgins, B. B. *Self-Contained Training Materials for Teacher Education.* Bloomington, Indiana National Center for the Development of Training Materials in Teacher Education, Indiana University, 1974.

Kaya, E., Gerhard, M., Staslewski, A., and Berenson, D. H. *Developing a Theory of Educational Practices for the Elementary School.* Norwalk, Conn.: Ford Foundation Fund for the Improvement of Education, 1967.

Kearney, N. C. *Elementary School Objectives.* New York: Russell Sage Foundation, 1953.

Lumsdaine, A. A. "Educational Technology, Programmed Learning and Instructional Science." In *Theories of Learning and Instruction,* National Society for the Study of Education, 63rd Yearbook, Part 1. Chicago: University of Chicago Press, 1964.

Mager, R. F. *Preparing Instructional Objectives.* San Francisco: Fearon Publishers, 1962.

Pfeiffer, Isobel L. "Teaching in Ability-Grouped English Classes: A Study of Verbal Interaction and Cognitive Goals." *Journal of Teacher Education,* 1966, *17*, No. 3.

Smith, W. I., and Moore, J. W. "Size of Step and Casing." *Psychological Reports,* 1962, *10*, 287-294.

SUMMARY
AND OVERVIEW

Instructional systems or training design is only one of many interventions necessary to achieve productivity goals. A comprehensive productivity systems design includes consulting, training, installation, follow-up, and support interventions. Within each of these interventions, there is a heavy emphasis upon evaluation: At what level did we achieve the productivity goals and individualized unit that we set out to achieve?

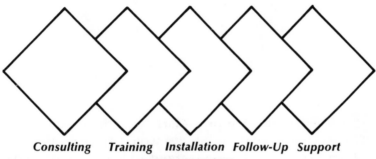

Consulting   Training   Installation   Follow-Up   Support
INTERVENTIONS

6

Training
Evaluation Skills

Basically, evaluation procedures ask the question: Did we achieve what we said we would achieve? We cannot practice any profession without asking this most fundamental of questions. We must know if what we do is valuable to others and ourselves. We must be shaped by the feedback that we get from our evaluations. Just as we ask the trainees to recycle the training process based upon the feedback they receive, so must we recycle the training process based upon the evaluations we receive. The evaluations are calculated to tell us whether we achieve our goals or not. If we fail to achieve our goals, the evaluation allows us to determine the deficits in our training approaches.

The most fundamental principle of evaluation is the principle of integrity: if we accomplish our training objectives, then we will have fulfilled our constructive intentions so that we remain integral. Systematic evaluations flow from systematic processes (Bass, 1975; Briggs, 1977; Carkhuff, 1969, 1971, 1983a; Sampe and Dressel, 1972). Nonsystematic evaluations are random by-products of nonsystematic processes. Thus, productive trainers measure what they attempted to accomplish (Ebel, 1965). While the indices of this measurement should be independent of the process, it is patently absurd to use measures that are totally unrelated to the process. We get what we train for—no more, no less (Brethower and Geary, 1976; Bronson, 1975; Carkhuff, 1983b; Carkhuff and Berenson, 1976; Mager and Beach, 1966; McCord, 1976; van Gigch, 1978). Generalization effects are serendipitous and unreplicable. Thus, our tests and measurements should reflect the process we have implemented to achieve our objectives. Ultimately, we must ask the basic evaluation question: Did we or did we not achieve the training objectives?

Principles of Evaluation

The training evaluation skill objective for this lesson is as follows:

The instructional trainees will evaluate the training programs by using systematic evaluation skills under formal and informal conditions and at levels that facilitate trainer skill improvement and trainee achievement.

Before you learn evaluation skills, you may want an index of your skills in this area. Perhaps you can outline how you would evaluate achievement of training skill objectives in your specialty content. Simply outline how you would measure goal achievement.

_____

_____

_____

_____

_____

Indexing Evaluation Skills

You should be pleased if you emphasized simple assessments of goal achievement: Did the trainees achieve the training skill objectives? Shy of this basic question, there are evaluations of task transfers, skill applications, content acquisition, and process movement. Together, these measures of process and outcome enable us to trace the movement of the trainees toward achieving the training objectives.

LEVELS OF EVALUATION	INDICES
5 **Goal Achievement:**	Did the trainees achieve the productivity goals?
4 **Task Transfers:**	Did the trainees transfer the skills to their real-life contextual tasks?
3 **Skill Applications:**	Did the trainees apply the skills to the training objectives?
2 **Content Acquisition:**	Did the trainees acquire the skill content?
1 **Process Movement:**	Did the trainees E-U-A the training delivery?

Overviewing Evaluation

Evaluating Process

The essential task in evaluating training process is to measure the trainees' movements in receiving the skills. The trainees' process movement can be measured according to their level of involving, exploring, understanding, acting, and recycling within the training experience. Usually, we begin with assessments of their recycling: Are the trainees involved in an ongoing E-U-A training process? If so, we move to evaluating acquisition, the next stage of evaluation. If trainees did not recycle the training process, we assess their level of acting. We continue in this manner until we have fully assessed the trainees' levels of involvement.

LEVELS OF PROCESS MOVEMENT	INDICES
5 Recycling:	Did the trainees recycle the E-U-A process within the training experience?
4 Acting:	Did the trainees act to achieve their goals within the training experience?
3 Understanding:	Did the trainees understand their goals within the training experience?
2 Exploring:	Did the trainees explore where they were in relation to the training experience?
1 Involving:	Did the trainees become involved in the training process by attending, observing, and listening?

Evaluating Process

For example, we might employ the following indices to assist us in discriminating the levels of trainee process movement in delivering our training content. You already know some sub-indices from your exposure to attending skills. Clearly, it would be helpful if the trainees have been taught what is expected of them. Trainers may advise trainees that these learning skills are in other reference materials (Carkhuff, 1984; Carkhuff and Berenson, 1981).

LEVELS OF PROCESS MOVEMENT	INDICES
5 Recycling:	Recycling Acting Recycling Understanding Recycling Exploring
4 Acting:	Implementing Programs Individualizing Programs Developing Programs
3 Understanding:	Defining Goals Personalizing Goals Setting Goals
2 Exploring:	Responding to Selves Diagnosing Selves Analyzing Experience
1 Involving:	Listening Observing Attending Physically

Evaluating Trainee Movement

You can use your evaluation skills to evaluate the effectiveness of our training delivery objectives in this volume. You may begin by evaluating your own process movement.

LEVELS OF PROCESS MOVEMENT	INDICES
5 **Recycling:**	Are you recycling the E-U-A process?
4 **Acting:**	Did you have a personalized training program?
3 **Understanding:**	Did you define your training goal?
2 **Exploring:**	Did you explore your training experience?
1 **Involving:**	Were you attentively involved in the training?

Again, you begin your assessments at the highest levels. If you have achieved them, you can move on to measuring acquisition, the next stage of evaluation. If you have not achieved them, you can move to the next highest level of process evaluation.

You may find it helpful to evaluate your trainees' process movements when you make your training delivery. Be sure that your training delivery emphasizes all of the training skills that facilitate the trainees' process movements, i.e., your *CPS* and *IPS*. That way you can stay attuned to the indices of trainee movement. Remember to begin by assessing recycling to work your way backward through the process levels or forward to our next evaluation stage. Indicate how you plan to assess each level of process movement.

LEVELS OF PROCESS MOVEMENT	INDICES
5 Recycling:	_____
	_____
4 Acting:	_____
	_____
3 Understanding:	_____
	_____
2 Exploring:	_____
	_____
1 Involving:	_____
	_____

Practicing Evaluating Process

Evaluating Acquisition

The essential task in evaluating the acquisition of content is to determine the level of skills and knowledge possessed by the trainees. These discriminations involve the levels of factual, conceptual, and principle knowledge. They emphasize the level of skill performance, including especially the level of skill steps performed. Usually, the evaluation begins with the skills: Can the trainees perform the skills? If they can, we move to measuring application, the next stage of evaluation. If they cannot, we discriminate the level of skill steps the trainees can perform. If the trainees have skill step deficits, we discriminate the levels of supportive knowledge they possess.

LEVELS OF ACQUISITION	INDICES
5 Skill Objective:	Can the trainees perform the skills?
4 Skill Steps:	Can the trainees perform the skill steps?
3 Principles:	Did the trainees acquire all of the principles?
2 Concepts:	Did the trainees acquire all of the conceptual knowledge?
1 Facts:	Did the trainees acquire all of the factual knowledge?

For example, we might employ the following indices to assist us in discriminating the levels of trainee acquisition after delivering our training skills content. You already know all of the definitions that you need in order to elaborate upon these indices.

LEVELS OF ACQUISITION	INDICES
5 **Skill Objective:**	Performance of objective
4 **Skill Steps:**	Steps to achieve objective
3 **Principles:**	Relationships and implications
2 **Concepts:**	Basic relationships
1 **Facts:**	Basic ingredients

Evaluating Trainee Skill Acquisition

Now use your evaluation skills to evaluate your own personal skill acquisition. Perhaps you can outline the basic skills involved in making a productive training delivery.

_____

_____

_____

_____

_____

_____

_____

Evaluating Personal Acquisition

Again, you may find it helpful to evaluate your own or your trainees' content acquisition after you have made your training delivery. Be sure to develop indices for the skill steps and supportive knowledge as well as the skill objective. Remember to begin with the assessment of the highest level of acquisition, i.e., the objective, and to branch from this discrimination.

LEVELS OF ACQUISITION	INDICES
5 Skill Objective:	_____
	_____
4 Skill Steps:	_____
	_____
3 Principles:	_____
	_____
2 Concepts:	_____
	_____
1 Facts:	_____
	_____

Practicing Evaluating Acquisition

Evaluating Application

The essential task in evaluating skill applications is to determine the level of application of the training objectives. These discriminations emphasize whether or not the trainees applied their skills to the dimensions of the skill objectives: components, functions, processes, conditions, and standards. Usually, we begin our assessment at the highest level: whether or not the trainees achieved standards of excellence in their application of the skill. We then branch forward to measuring transfer, the next stage of evaluation, or backward to the previous level of skill application, depending upon the discriminations we make.

LEVELS OF APPLICATION	INDICES
5 Standards:	Did the trainees apply their skills to the intended levels of excellence?
4 Conditions:	Did the trainees apply their skills to the basic conditions of objectives?
3 Processes:	Did the trainees apply their skills to the basic methods of objectives?
2 Functions:	Did the trainees apply their skills to the basic purposes of objectives?
1 Components:	Did the trainees apply their skills to the basic ingredients of objectives?

Evaluating Application

For example, we might employ the following indices to assist in discriminating the levels of trainee application to training skills objectives. These indices constitute a review of the steps used in defining skill objectives.

LEVELS OF APPLICATION	INDICES
5 **Standards:**	How well is it being done?
4 **Conditions:**	Where and when is it being done?
3 **Processes:**	How is it being done?
2 **Functions:**	What is being done?
1 **Components:**	Who and what is involved?

Evaluating Trainee Skill Application

You can also evaluate your level of application of the training skill objective. Take one or more of the following tasks and develop a training delivery plan: delivery tasks, supervisory tasks, and/or management tasks. Then outline how you would use your training management skills in implementing the training delivery plan.

TRAINING DELIVERY PLAN:

_____

_____

_____

_____

_____

TRAINING MANAGEMENT SKILLS:

_____

_____

_____

_____

_____

Evaluating Personal Application

Again, you may find it helpful to evaluate your own or your trainees' skill applications after having acquired the content. Be sure you have indices for all the dimensions of the training skill objective. Remember to begin with the highest level discrimination and branch from there.

LEVELS OF APPLICATION	INDICES
5 Standards:	_____
	_____
4 Conditions:	_____
	_____
3 Processes:	_____
	_____
2 Functions:	_____
	_____
1 Components:	_____
	_____

Practicing Evaluating Application

Evaluating Transfer

The task in evaluating transfer is directly analogous to that of evaluating application. The difference is that the skill application is planned and the transfer is not planned. Nevertheless, even in a work setting, there are a variety of opportunities for assessing task transfers. Again, we branch from the discriminations of the highest levels of transfer.

LEVELS OF TRANSFER	INDICES
5 Standards:	Did the trainees transfer their skills to the measures of excellence in task performance?
4 Conditions:	Did the trainees transfer their skills to basic contexts of task performance?
3 Processes:	Did the trainees transfer their skills to basic methods of task performance?
2 Functions:	Did the trainees transfer their skills to basic purposes of task performance?
1 Components:	Did the trainees transfer their skills to basic ingredients of task performance?

Evaluating Transfer

For example, we might employ the following indices to assist in discriminating the levels of trainee transfer to tasks other than the training skills objectives, i.e., tasks involving employees or bosses or other trainers, officials, or family members. Again, we would employ the same essential dimensions of skill objectives.

LEVELS OF TRANSFER	INDICES
5 **Standards:**	How well?
4 **Conditions:**	Where and when?
3 **Processes:**	How?
2 **Functions:**	What?
1 **Components:**	Who?

Evaluating Trainee Task Transfer

You can also evaluate your level of transfer to your real-life contextual tasks. Select an area of your specialty content and outline a training delivery plan. Then outline how you would implement the plan by using your training management skills.

TRAINING DELIVERY PLAN:

_____

_____

_____

_____

_____

TRAINING MANAGEMENT SKILLS:

_____

_____

_____

_____

_____

Evaluating Personal Transfer

You might find it helpful to evaluate your own or your trainees' skill transfers to real-life tasks. Be sure you have indices for all the dimensions to be used to measure task performance. Begin with the highest level discrimination.

LEVELS OF TRANSFER	INDICES
5 Standards:	_____
	_____
4 Conditions:	_____
	_____
3 Processes:	_____
	_____
2 Functions:	_____
	_____
1 Components:	_____
	_____

Practicing Evaluating Transfer

Evaluating Achievement

The essential task in evaluating goal achievement is making the following basic discrimination. Did the trainees achieve the original training goal? In addition, we may assess how productive the trainers were in achieving the goal: Were the trainees efficient and/or effective in achieving the goal or were the trainees inefficient and/or ineffective in achieving the goal? In evaluating levels of achievement, it may be most facilitative to determine: first, whether or not the goal was achieved (Level 3); second, if so, whether it was achieved efficiently and/or effectively (Levels 4 and 5); and third, if not, whether it was deficit in efficiency and/or effectiveness (Levels 1 and 2).

LEVELS OF ACHIEVEMENT	INDICES
5 Productive:	Were the trainees efficient *and* effective in achieving the goal?
4 Additive:	Were the trainees particularly efficient *or* effective in achieving the goal?
3 Objective:	Did the trainees achieve the target goal?
2 Subtractive:	Were the trainees inefficient *or* ineffective in achieving the goal?
1 Nonproductive:	Were the trainees inefficient *and* ineffective in achieving the goal?

Evaluating Achievement

For example, we might employ the following indices to assist in discriminating the levels of trainee achievement of the training goal. In other words, we are evaluating both the results and the resources expended. In so doing, we would employ the following indices:

LEVELS OF ACHIEVEMENT	INDICES
5 Productive:	Overachieved in results; *and* Achieved results before the dead-line with minimal resource expenditures.
4 Additive:	Overachieved; *or* Achieved results before the dead-line with minimal resource expenditures.
3 Objective:	Achieved results; on time.
2 Subtractive:	Underachieved in results; *or* Achieved results late with maximum resource expenditures.
1 Nonproductive:	Underachieved in results; *and* Achieved results late with maximum resource expenditures.

Evaluating Trainee Goal Achievement

Now you can evaluate whether you achieved the personal goals that you set before training. Simply review your personal goals and determine to what degree you achieved them.

PERSONAL GOALS:

_____

_____

_____

_____

_____

Evaluating Personal Goal Achievement

Again, you might evaluate yourself on your trainees' levels of goal achievement. Begin with discrimination of goal achievement and branch to incremental or decremental levels of productivity.

LEVELS OF ACHIEVEMENT	INDICES
5 Productive:	_____
	_____
4 Additive:	_____
	_____
3 Objective:	_____
	_____
2 Subtractive:	_____
	_____
1 Nonproductive:	_____
	_____

Practicing Evaluating Achievement

Exercising

We can apply the evaluation skills in a variety of living, learning, and working contexts. However, in this regard, it is important to remember that we can most systematically assess only those programs that we have designed, developed, and implemented systematically. We can teach our trainees to evaluate their own training programs' processes and outcomes: process movement, content acquisition, skill application, task transfers, and goal achievements.

SKILL OBJECTIVE:

> *Trainees will evaluate training programs by using systematic evaluation procedures in training and at levels that provide them feedback to shape the training-learning processes.*

PROCESS: _____

_____

ACQUISITION: _____

_____

APPLICATION: _____

_____

TRANSFER: _____

_____

ACHIEVEMENT: _____

_____

Exercising Evaluation Skills

You may wish to repeat practicing your evaluation skills. Apply the evaluation skills to living and learning contexts. Develop your process, acquisition, application, transfer, and achievement measures.

SKILL OBJECTIVE:

_____

_____

_____

PROCESS: _____

_____

ACQUISITION: _____

_____

APPLICATION: _____

_____

TRANSFER: _____

_____

ACHIEVEMENT: _____

_____

Repeating Evaluation Skills

Try to make a variety of new living, learning, and working applications of your evaluation skills within your specialty skill content.

LIVING: _____

_____

_____

LEARNING: _____

_____

_____

WORKING: _____

_____

_____

Applying Evaluation Skills

Summarizing

Perhaps you can now take some aspect of your specialty content and outline how you would evaluate its goal achievement. Simply outline the measures of goal achievement you would employ.

If you are able to evaluate your specialty content achievements, then we are confident that you will be able to pursue our evaluation objective throughout your professional career:

> *The instructional trainees will evaluate the training process by using systematic evaluation skills under formal and informal conditions and at levels that facilitate trainer skill improvement and trainee achievement.*

Indexing Evaluation Skills

Again, we can evaluate systematically only that which we have designed, developed, and implemented systematically. We see that training is initiated with training goals. Therefore, training must in the final analysis be evaluated by the level of achievement of these goals. Similarly, the other levels of process and outcome are related according to their systematic development and evaluation.

PHASES OF DEVELOPMENT	LEVELS OF EVALUATION
Goals Established	5 Goal Achievement
Tasks Analyzed	4 Task Transfers
Skills Objectified	3 Skill Applications
Content Developed	2 Content Acquisition
Process Delivered	1 Process Movement

Summarizing Evaluation Skills

In the end, we either achieve our goals or we do not. The pursuit of the goals is what shapes our integrity. When we learn to achieve our goals with maximum efficiency and effectiveness, then we may say that we are productive in that specific area. We may recycle our efforts in other areas. As we are shaped by our evaluations, we move increasingly toward becoming more and more productive: using minimal resources to achieve maximum results. We build our integrity, pure and directionful, cell-by-cell, in this manner. Increasingly, we develop an X-ray vision that enables us to see things in sharp relief. Always, we elevate our visions of the ideals to be accomplished as we face and answer the basic anxieties of human existence: Are we good enough?

References

Bass, B. *Training in Industry: The Management of Learning.* Monterey, Calif.: Brooks/Cole, 1975.

Briggs, L. *Instructional Design.* Englewood Cliffs, N.J.: Educational Technology Publications, 1977.

Brethower, K. S., and Geary, G. A. "Evaluating Training." *NSPI Improving Human Performance Quarterly,* 1976.

Bronson, R. K. *Interservice Procedures for Instructional Systems Development.* Tallahassee, Fla.: Center for Educational Technology, 1975.

Carkhuff, R. R. *Helping and Human Relations. Volumes I and II.* New York: Holt, Rinehart and Winston, 1969.

Carkhuff, R. R. *The Development of Human Resources.* New York: Holt, Rinehart and Winston. 1971.

Carkhuff, R. R. *Sources of Human Productivity.* Amherst, Mass.: Human Resource Development Press, 1983.(a)

Carkhuff, R. R. "Assessing Intervention Outcomes." In *The Training and Development Sourcebook,* edited by C. E. Schneier, and D. Laird. Amherst, Mass.: Human Resource Development Press, 1983.(b)

Carkhuff, R. R. *Human Processing.* Amherst, Mass.: Human Resource Development Press, in press, 1984

Carkhuff, R. R., and Berenson, B. G. *Teaching As Treatment.* Amherst, Mass.: Human Resource Development Press, 1976.

Carkhuff, R. R., and Berenson, D. H. *The Skilled Teacher.* Amherst, Mass.: Human Resurce Development Press, 1981.

Ebel, R. L. *Measuring Educational Achievement.* Englewood Cliffs, N.J.: Prentice-Hall, 1965.

Mager, R. F., and Beach, K. M. *Developing Vocational Instruction*. San Francisco: Fearon-Pitman, 1966.

McCord, B. "Job Instruction." Chapter in *Training and Development Handbook*. Washington, D.C.: American Society for Training and Development, 1976.

Sampe, J. L., and Dressel, P. L. "Evaluating Outcomes of Instruction." Chapter in *Institutional Research in the University*, edited by P.L. Dressel. Washington, D.C.: Jossey-Bass, 1972.

van Gigch, J. P. *Applied General Systems Theory*. New York: Harper and Row, 1978.

7

Productive Interventions in the Age of Information

Productive development and training is systematic development and training. It involves designing and implementing instructional interventions to achieve the productivity goals. It emphasizes the training delivery skills that enable trainers to prepare and make the training delivery. It emphasizes the achievement by the trainees of the original productivity goals. In sum, productive development and training emphasizes the systematic achievement of productivity goals.

To be sure, instructional interventions are one of a series of interventions necessary to achieve significant and lasting gains (Carkhuff, 1983, 1984b; Carkhuff, Fisher, Cannon, Friel and Pierce, 1984) (see Figure 7-1). In comprehensive productivity interventions, the consulting intervention precedes the instructional intervention. The consulting intervention provides the productivity goals that are refined to drive the instructional intervention.

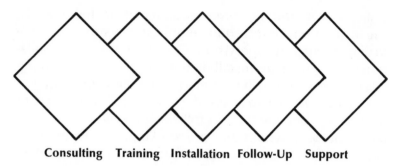

Consulting   Training   Installation   Follow-Up   Support

Figure 7-1. Comprehensive Productivity Systems
Intervention

In addition, a number of interventions are necessary
to insure the success of the instructional intervention. The
installation intervention systematically installs the purposes
of the instructional intervention. The follow-up intervention insures the lasting benefits for both the trainees and
their recipients. The support intervention provides the
lasting support for the purposes of the instructional
intervention.

Together, these systems interventions comprise the
interventions necessary to achieve productivity goals. The
consulting intervention tells the trainees what the productivity goals are. The instructional intervention teaches the
trainees what they need to do to achieve the goals. The
installation intervention guides the trainees in implementing their newly achieved skills. The follow-up intervention
monitors the performance of the trainees and their recipients. The support intervention creates the facilitative work
complex for supporting the changes that have been
installed.

From another view, we may conceive of these interventions in terms of the various levels of functions in a productivity system. The consulting intervention addresses

policy makers and high level decision makers. Increasingly, the instructional intervention emphasizes various levels of management and supervision. Consequently, the installation usually involves installing the purpose of the training intervention with delivery personnel. Follow-up interventions take place at two levels: the trainers following up with the trainees, and the trainees following up with the delivery personnel with whom they are working. Finally, the support intervention emphasizes transforming the work milieu to facilitate productivity.

No one intervention is more powerful than any other intervention. Each by itself is incomplete. Thus, for example, the instructional intervention is unrelated to productivity goals if a consulting intervention has not preceded it. Similarly, the lasting effects of the instructional intervention become problematic if the resultant installation, follow-up, or support interventions are not systematically designed and implemented. Indeed, if we must choose between the instructional and the follow-up interventions, then we might choose the follow-up intervention because it emphasizes the criteria on which the personnel will be monitored.

Similarly, within the instructional interventions, each station is incomplete without the others. Thus, training deliveries that are unrelated to instructional design are unrelated to productive outcomes. Likewise, training preparations that are unrelated to training delivery are unrelated to productive outcomes.

Productivity Systems Design

It is in the context of comprehensive productivity systems design that we view the necessary systems interventions. All comprehensive productivity systems interventions begin with consulting systems design. The missions of the policy makers and the goals of the decision makers drive all other systems interventions. Ultimately, the interventions will be evaluated on the basis of how well they achieve the decision maker's original goals.

Consulting Systems Design

The basic systems and technologies of consulting interventions are presented in Figure 7-2. As can be seen, the consultants work with the policy makers to do the following: define the organizational mission, develop the strategic goals, make the strategic decisions, develop the strategic plans, deliver the strategic plans to the decision makers, and evaluate the decision makers' refinement of the organizational mission and goals.

The consulting systems design refines the decision makers' images of the organizational goals. These organizational goals are the stimuli to the instigation of instructional systems design. These goals direct the development of all subsequent intervention design.

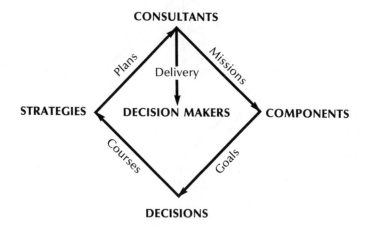

Figure 7-2. Consulting Intervention Design

Instructional Systems Design

The basic systems technologies of instructional interventions are presented in Figure 7-3. The trainer works with the target units to refine the productivity goals into individualized unit goals; analyze the context to develop tasks to achieve the unit goals; specify the training skill objectives that comprise the tasks; develop the skill content to achieve the training skill objectives; develop and make a delivery to the trainees; and evaluate the trainees' levels of achievement of the unit goals.

The instructional systems design defines the tasks to be performed to achieve the unit goals. The objectives and tasks are the stimuli to initiating the installation systems design.

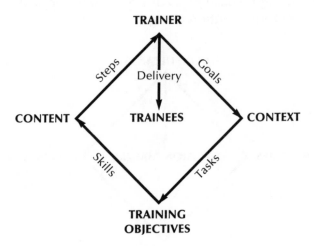

Figure 7-3. Instructional Intervention Design

Installation Systems Design

The basic systems and technologies of the installation intervention are presented in Figure 7-4. The installation intervener works with personnel in the working context as
follows: to further refine and individualize unit goals, to
further define the tasks to be implemented, to design the
plans to install, to make the installation, and to evaluate
the installation.

The installation systems design defines the tasks to be
performed to implement the functions of the instructional
intervention. In so doing, it stimulates the follow-up interventions necessary to insure task performance.

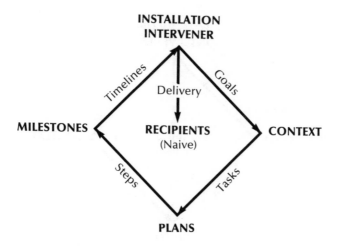

Figure 7-4. Installation Intervention Design

Follow-Up Systems Design

The basic systems and technologies of the follow-up intervention are presented in Figure 7.5. The follow-up intervener works with the trainee-recipients of the instructional intervention to accomplish the following follow-up tasks: develop individualized goals, refine the tasks to be performed, refine the steps and timelines to be accomplished, make the delivery of the modified plans to the trainee-recipients, and evaluate the trainee-recipients' performances.

In turn, the trainee-recipients conduct their own follow-up intervention to insure the performance of the recipients of their installation. Together, the trainer and trainee follow-up interventions stimulate the support interventions necessary to facilitate lasting change.

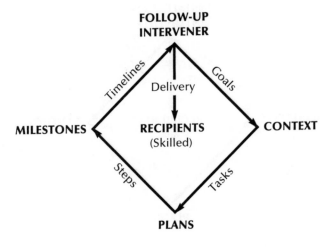

Figure 7-5. Follow-Up Intervention Design

Support Systems Design

The basic systems and technologies of the support inter-vention are presented in Figure 7-6. The support intervener works with the different levels of management and super-vision to accomplish the following support tasks: indi-vidualize support goals, refine the supportive tasks to be performed, define the plans to be implemented, deliver the plans and evaluate the performance of support personnel.

The support intervention is designed to provide the lasting support for the installation intervention. It recycles the evaluation of the achievement of all individualized unit goals and ultimately the original productivity goals.

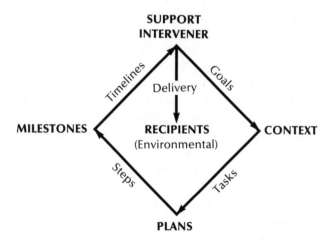

Figure 7-6. Support Intervention Design

Summary and Conclusions

In summary, training delivery skills are part of instructional systems design. They emphasize the preparation and making of the training delivery. They are derived from the individualized unit goals and the contextual tasks needed to achieve these goals.

The preparation of the training delivery emphasizes the following instructional or training design tasks: defining the training objectives, developing the delivery content, and developing the delivery plan. Training delivery emphasizes the following tasks: making the training delivery, and evaluating the training delivery. Together, the training delivery skills emphasize the definition and achievement of training objectives that lead to the task performance which enables us to achieve our productivity goals.

In turn, the instructional systems design is part of productivity systems design. Productivity systems design emphasizes the design of all of the interventions needed to accomplish the organizational mission and component productivity goals. These systems include the consulting systems design that leads to instructional systems design. They also include the installation, follow-up, and support systems designs that insure the achievement of individualized objectives, unit goals, and the organizational mission.

Training delivery skills must be viewed in the context of instructional systems design. In general, training delivery skills are the necessary but not sufficient condition of instructional systems design. We get what we train for—no more, no less!

Instructional systems design must be viewed in the context of comprehensive productivity systems design. In general, instructional systems design is a necessary but not sufficient condition of productivity systems design. We get what we plan for—no more, no less!

Productivity systems design must be viewed in the context of comprehensive resource systems design. In general, organizational productivity goals are a necessary but not sufficient condition of resource, economic, political, and educational systems designs. We get what we pay for—no more, no less!

We pay for our own exemplary performance with the same currency we pay for organizational, community, regional, national, or global productivity: our knowledge of systems design; our skills in developing and implementing technologies; our commitment to learning and teaching; our concern for communicating and disseminating; our inclusive relationships with our worlds; our focused motivation in our missions; and our energy resources to accomplish our mission.

The currencies of the Information Age are the ideas generated by the human brain. The profitability of the Information Age is measured in lasting human benefits. The driving force of the Information Age is the individual exemplar who is a living embodiment of all of the available models, systems, and technologies to accomplish any reasonable human purpose (Carkhuff, 1984a).

The core ingredient in all productivity achievement is the individual human. Each healthy human brain possesses 100 billion neurons—"state-of-the-art" computers programmed in the languages of electronics and chemistry. Each healthy human brain possesses the power to out-produce all humanity—historically and existentially.

In conclusion, all humans are potentially universes unto themselves, capable of reaching the corners of the external, physical universes; capable of defining the goals of their internal, phenomenal universes. Human success depends upon the human processing skills (Carkhuff, 1984b) and technical design skills people learn in order to unlock those universes.

References

Carkhuff, R. R. *Sources of Human Productivity.* Amherst, Mass.: Human Resource Development Press, 1983.

Carkhuff, R. R. *The Exemplar: The Exemplary Performer in the Age of Productivity.* Amherst, Mass.: Human Resource Development Press, 1984.(a)

Carkhuff, R. R. *Human Processing.* Amherst, Mass.: Human Resource Development Press, in press, 1984.(b)

Carkhuff, R. R.; Fisher, S. G.; Cannon, J. R.; Friel, T. W. and Pierce, R. M. *Instructional Systems Design. Volumes I and II.* Amherst, Mass.: Human Resource Development Press, 1984.

INDEX

A

Argyris, C., 85, 122
Aspy, D.N., 85, 122
Attending, 88 ff.
    physically, 89
    practicing, 92
Ausebel, D., 17, 29

B

Bass, B., 161, 190
Beach, K.M., 51, 83, 161, 191
Berdele, W.E., 85, 123
Berenson, B.G., 161, 165, 190
Berenson, D.H., 51, 82, 83, 85, 122, 125, 154, 155, 156
Berenson, S.R., 51, 82, 125, 154
Berliner, D.C., 125, 154
Bloom, B.S., 17, 29, 85, 122, 125, 155
Brethower, K.S., 161, 190
Briggs, L., 161, 190
Bronson, R.K., 161, 190

C

Campbell, J.P., 51, 82
Cannon, J.R., 26, 29, 30, 45, 192, 202
Carkhuff, R.R., 5, 6, 8, 26, 29, 30, 45, 51, 82, 85, 122, 125, 155, 161, 165, 190, 192, 201, 202
Clark, D.C., 51, 82, 125, 155
Content processing skills, 37, 50 ff.
    applying, 78
    exercising, 76, 77
    indexing, 52, 79
    in the exercise, 142
    in the overview, 134
    in the presentation, 138
    in the review, 129
    in the summary, 146

658.3124
C277

118 800

Carkhuff & Pierce :

T.D.S. : Making the training delivery

DATE DUE

GAYLORD			PRINTED IN U.S.A.